40 Days and Nights on the Camino de Santiago

A Pilgrimage for Finding

CLARITY, RENEWAL, AND HEALING

Kevin Wittmayer

Morehouse Publishing
19 East 34th Street
New York, NY 10016
www.churchpublishing.org

Morehouse Publishing is an imprint of Church Publishing Incorporated.

Cover design by David Baldeosingh Rotstein
Typeset by Westchester Publishing Services

ISBN 978-1-64065-970-4 (paperback)
ISBN 978-1-64065-983-4 (eBook)

Library of Congress Control Number: 2025951405

Dedication

To my wife Pamela, whom I couldn't imagine walking through life without. You have been a co-laborer in God's vineyard with me, always walking beside me. When God has asked us to go, you have always responded, "Here we are, Lord, send us."

To my mother, who would have loved to have lived long enough to see this book published. She was my first fan, and as a teacher, she instilled in me a love for books and reading. She often would say to me as a child, "Books are our friends."

To my daughters Kristel and Melissa, you are the joy of my life, and I can't imagine life without you. It is first and foremost for you and your children and grandchildren that I write this book. It is my prayer that through its words, you might see Jesus and experience God's love for you.

Contents

Purgation

Dying to Self

Resurrection

Preface

In the intervening years since I walked the Camino de Santiago, I've had the opportunity to share the experience of my pilgrimage with church groups, civic organizations, and friends. With PowerPoint in hand, I've recounted the stories and shown the photos of my pilgrimage, trying, in some small way, to invite others into those days of beauty, struggle, and grace. Recently, in preparation for a presentation, I did something I hadn't done in the many years since my pilgrimage: I sat down and read through my journal entries written while walking the Camino. As I turned each page, I was transported back to those sacred days, and I found myself walking the Camino once again—this time through memory and reflection.

That experience prompted me to digitize my journals. I wanted those thoughts and reflections to be more accessible—not only for myself but for my children, grandchildren, and descendants yet to come. As an amateur genealogist, I know how elusive the lives and characters of our ancestors can be. If one of my great-great-grandchildren ever wonders what kind of person I was, I hope this offers at least a small window into my heart and faith.

Yet as I transcribed my journals, I realized I am more than the details of a daily walk or the emotions captured in a fleeting moment.

I'm also an Episcopal priest, a person whose life has been deeply shaped by faith, so it was important to me that the spiritual dimension of my life be present alongside the travelogue. So, I began to write a reflection for each day of the Camino—drawing not only from the experience itself but from the perspective and spiritual growth that time, distance, and continued pilgrimage through life have provided me. Each day's entry is divided into two parts. First is a transcription of my original journal entry. I have edited that entry where sensitivity for the privacy of others is warranted or to provide greater clarity for the reader. I have also attempted to be gender neutral when referring to God wherever possible, without it appearing clumsy. The exception to this general principle is in the quotation of Scripture, where I have left the translations as received.

The second part is a spiritual reflection based on that day's journal and my memory of that day, along with a Scripture passage, questions to encourage personal contemplation by the reader, and a concluding prayer.

I've never imagined myself as someone who would write a devotional. Others, I'm sure, possess greater theological prowess and can provide greater insights into the Scripture passages included. What I share—and what I admire most in the Psalms—is a raw and honest faith. Like David and the other psalmists, I make space in these pages for both joy and disappointment, for clarity and confusion, for moments of disorientation and the grace of reorientation. This devotional is both a travelogue and an unvarnished window into my soul.

My hope—beyond simply preserving this for my family—is that others might find in these reflections a companion for their journey. Perhaps in my struggles of faith, someone may feel less alone. Perhaps in moments of joy and connection, another might catch a glimmer of hope for their life as well.

For many years, when people asked how long it took me to walk the Camino Frances, I told them my Camino lasted thirty-four days. As I read my journal, I realized I began recording entries three days before I started walking and continued for three days after reaching Santiago de Compostela. Forty days—an unmistakably biblical number. As any student of Scripture knows, forty signifies a time of testing, transformation, and encounter with the divine.

This Camino was just that for me. Aside from my marriage and the birth of my daughters, it was possibly the most important and formative experience of my life. Wherever I went, I bumped into grace: in strangers' kindness, unexpected beauty, hard conversations, silent prayers, and moments of both deep joy and disorientation. I didn't always recognize it right away, but grace was always there, meeting me on the road.

Because the journey spans forty days, this devotional could serve the reader well as a spiritual companion for the forty days of the liturgical season of Lent—a time when many Christians reflect more intentionally on their own path, struggles, and the presence of God in the wilderness. Wherever this devotional finds you—on the road, at home, or somewhere in between—I pray it brings you courage, hope, and a deeper awareness of God's grace.

Buen Camino!

Acknowledgments

This book was born on a dusty trail in northern Spain, but its heart was shaped long before I ever set foot on the Camino. I am deeply grateful for the grace that met me step by step—grace that came in the form of silence, strangers, shared bread, and the still, small voice of God. Thank you to the many churches, civic organizations, and friends who have allowed me to share my Camino with them over the years.

To Pamela, my beloved companion of forty-eight years: Your love, presence, and willingness to join me on the road—both literally and spiritually—has been the deepest grace of all. Thank you for giving me space to walk, and for letting me walk you into the story when the time was right.

To the pilgrims I met along the way, who walked with me—whether for a mile or a lifetime—thank you. Your companionship, encouragement, and prayers gave shape to this journey and voice to these reflections. I carry your stories with reverence. Though many of your names never made it into this manuscript, your faces and kindnesses are written on my heart.

I also wish to express my deep gratitude to Bishop C. Andrew Doyle for his pastoral guidance and encouragement to take advantage of a sabbatical. To the Episcopal Diocese of Texas, thank you for the sabbatical grant that made this pilgrimage possible.

Special thanks to those who labored through early drafts of this book, offering encouragement, insight, and the occasional red pen. The Reverend Shanna Neff, after reading the draft of the first four days, suggested I turn my Camino reflections into this devotional. My thanks to Lori and Stuart MacDonald, who have also walked the Camino and offered steady encouragement for the writing of this book from its conception.

Above all, I give thanks to God, whose grace met me at every turn on the Camino and continues to meet me on the road of life.

Separation from Home

DAY 1

The Journey Begins

I can't believe how difficult it was to leave Pamela and everything familiar behind today. I've been looking forward to this trip and this sabbatical for months, yet when the moment arrived, I was filled with unexpected anxiety—anxiety about my physical condition, about the long hours of solitude ahead, about the inner battles I'll likely face on the Camino. It's strange how anticipation, which I'd imagined would bring excitement, has instead brought this heavy weight.

As I sit with this anxiety, I can't help but wonder: Did Jesus feel something similar after his baptism, when he was driven into the wilderness? Was there a moment of tension, of uncertainty, before he faced the great challenges ahead? It's a strange comfort to think that perhaps even he knew what it was like to be gripped by fear and anxiety before his journey began.

Already, I've been invited to let go in so many ways. The afternoon was filled with frustration—my phone app wasn't working properly. I couldn't help but wonder if this small hiccup was somehow meant to be. Could it be that this is a subtle nudge to detach, to not lean on the comfort of easy calls home, to resist the pull of staying tethered to everything familiar?

The stress of the travel day didn't ease my anxiety either. The flight from Dallas to Boston was delayed by an hour, meaning there's a good chance I'll miss my connection to Madrid. If that happens, I'll spend the night in Boston while my backpack possibly continues to San Sebastián. If I start the Camino late, maybe, just maybe, by God's grace, I'll miss the rain that's predicted for Saint-Jean-Pied-de-Port on Saturday. For now, here I am with a heart full of questions and a mind already racing toward what comes next.

The God Who Sends

Now the LORD said to Abram, "Go from your country and your kindred and your father's house to the land that I will show you. I will make of you a great nation, and I will bless you and make your name great, so that you will be a blessing. I will bless those who bless you, and the one who curses you I will curse; and in you all the families of the earth shall be blessed." So Abram went, as the LORD had told him.

—Genesis 12:1–4a

We see from the earliest chapters of Genesis that God has always been a sending God. From the moment God calls Abraham to leave his homeland and go to a place he has never seen, God begins a long pattern of calling ordinary people into extraordinary journeys. Later, God sends Moses to stand before Pharaoh and demand the release of God's enslaved people—an act filled with confrontation, danger, and divine purpose. Throughout the Old Testament, we see prophets sent to deliver difficult, often unwelcome messages to God's people. Isaiah, Jeremiah, Ezekiel, and Amos—just to name a few—were messengers not only of comfort, but of correction and hope rooted in repentance.

This divine sending doesn't end in the Old Testament. In the New Testament, John the Baptist is sent to prepare the way for the coming Messiah. Jesus himself is sent—the incarnate Son of God—driven by the Spirit into the wilderness to face temptation at the very start of his ministry. Later, in Luke 10, we see Jesus sending his disciples out two by two—a kind of spiritual apprenticeship—to the very places Jesus himself intended to go. The word *apostle* literally means "sent one," underscoring the fact that to follow Jesus is to live as one who is sent.

In the story of Jesus in the wilderness, we're not told exactly how Jesus felt as he began his public ministry. Later, in the Garden of Gethsemane, the Gospels give us a vivid window into his inner turmoil. On the night before his crucifixion, Jesus pleads with the Father to take the cup of suffering from him, not once, but three times. Still, he surrenders with the words, "not my will but yours be done" (Luke 22:42). Even after this act of surrender, his anguish wasn't over. Hanging on the cross, Jesus cries out, "My God, my God, why have you forsaken me?" (Matthew 27:46), revealing the depth of the emotional and spiritual weight he bore.

It's often said that courage is not an absence of fear but the willingness to move forward despite fear. Abraham showed that kind of courage when he left everything familiar for an unknown land. The prophets showed it when they spoke truth in hostile times. Jesus showed it most fully when he set his face toward the cross. Honestly, should we be expected to do anything less than move out in faith when we decide to follow a God who sent his own son into the world?

So, while the fear and anxiety I felt as I boarded my plane for Spain may not compare to what they faced, it is a part of the same spiritual dynamic. What I share in my decision to walk the Camino was the courage to step into the unknown, believing that God goes with us. Like those before us, we cling to the promise that God's presence will sustain us, and that through faith and obedience, we will experience God's blessing, just as Abraham did.

Reflection Questions:

1. What is God asking you to leave behind in this season of life, and what fears or attachments make that difficult?
2. Where might God be sending you, not necessarily geographically, but relationally, vocationally, or spiritually?
3. What blessings have you experienced in the past when you chose to trust and follow God into the unknown?

God of Abraham, God of the wilderness,
you call us to leave what is familiar and step into the unknown.
Today, that call feels heavier than I expected.
Anxiety presses in, questions crowd my thoughts,
and even small disruptions feel like tests of trust.

Yet you are the God who goes before me—
who sent Abraham from home, who sent Jesus into solitude,
who sends each of us into places where you are already at work.

Meet me here, in this uneasy beginning.
Give me courage not because I feel brave,
but because I believe you walk with me.

Help me to let go, to trust the detours,
and to believe that blessing lies somewhere ahead—
not in certainty, but in obedience.

Amen.

DAY 2

A Detour in Boston

The adventure has begun, though not quite as I had expected. I missed my connecting flight to Madrid, so here I am, spending an extra day in Boston, courtesy of American Airlines. It's funny, what I thought would be a frustrating setback now feels like the beginning of the pilgrimage in a way that's beyond my own planning. Perhaps this is how it was meant to be, according to God's plan rather than my own.

The silver lining is that by starting a day later, I'll miss the rainstorm that is forecasted for Saint-Jean-Pied-de-Port, France, on Saturday. So, in the end, it all works out. "God is good, all the time. All the time, God is good." Today, I spent some time at the John F. Kennedy Presidential Library, soaking in a bit of American history. Later, I wandered over to Quincy Market, but all in all, it was a relatively quiet day. It's almost as though the journey is starting with a pause, a moment of rest before the real challenge begins.

Thresholds of Trust

As Jesus passed along the Sea of Galilee, he saw Simon and his brother Andrew casting a net into the sea—for they were fishermen. And Jesus said to them, "Follow me and I will make you fish for people." And immediately they left their nets and followed him. As he went a little farther, he saw James son of Zebedee and his brother John, who were in their boat mending the nets. Immediately he called them; and they left their father Zebedee in the boat with the hired men, and followed him.

—Mark 1:16–20

Though I hadn't yet placed a foot on the Camino, the pilgrimage had already begun. Pilgrimage always begins in unfamiliar places—in liminal spaces. Boston, with its strange sights, unfamiliar sounds, and countless strangers, is far from anything that resembles Texas. It felt foreign. So, the anxiety I felt on day one of this journey carries into day two. Perhaps that, too, is by God's design.

As much as God is a sending God, God is also a God who meets us in liminal spaces. The word *liminal* comes from the Latin *limen*, meaning threshold. Scripture is full of these thresholds—Moses meets God on the mountain, Elijah in a cave, David while fleeing for his life, Jesus in the wilderness, the disciples on the shores of the Sea of Galilee, and Paul on the way to Damascus in his blindness. Again and again, God shows up when we step beyond what is known and into what is not known.

I grew up in the Baptist church, studied at Oral Roberts University, and now serve as an Episcopal priest. Who says God doesn't have a sense of humor? I've experienced the full spectrum of worship styles and traditions. Yet in every context, the most powerful moments of worship have been those when I released control—let go of the familiar—and simply trusted what God was doing. In the Episcopal liturgy, one of those moments comes during the singing of the Sanctus. I remember learning during my seminary studies that this is considered one of, if not the, holiest moments of our liturgy.

The words come from Isaiah's call to prophetic ministry in Isaiah 6—a profoundly liminal moment. Angels fly, a burning coal touches Isaiah's lips, and he cries out in recognition of his unworthiness before God. When we sing "Holy, holy, holy Lord, God of power and might, heaven and earth are full of your glory," we step into that same threshold. It's not, however, just the words that carry us—it's their context. We are invited to sing the Sanctus with these words, "joining our voices with Angels and Archangels and with all the company of heaven, who for ever sing this hymn." In that moment, we are not just in our pews—we're with the saints, our ancestors, and the generations to come, worshipping God with one voice.

It is in these moments when I am invited to press into God, I am also asked to surrender. Surrender my plans, my expectations, my control—and to simply trust. I'm invited like Isaiah, when God asks who he can send, to respond, "Here am I, send me." Spending a day in Boston, on the day when I had planned to begin my Camino, felt like a disruption. Perhaps it was not a detour. Perhaps it was an invitation—God's invitation—to trust more deeply, listen more closely, and rest more fully in God's presence.

I can't help but believe that at that moment in my journey, Jesus was saying to me, like he did to the disciples, drop everything and follow me. That's an invitation I wanted to accept.

Reflection Questions:

1. Where in your life are you currently standing on a threshold—between what is known and what is unknown? How might God be inviting you to step forward in trust?
2. Can you recall a time when a disruption or delay turned out to be a sacred invitation from God? What did you learn through it?
3. What "nets"—plans, expectations, or comforts—might God be asking you to lay down so that you can follow more freely?

Disturb us, Lord, when we are too pleased with ourselves, when our dreams have come true because we dreamed too little, when we arrived safely because we sailed too close to the shore. Disturb us, Lord, when with the abundance of things we possess, we have lost our thirst for the waters of life; having fallen in love with life, we have ceased to dream of eternity, and in our efforts to build a new earth, we have allowed our vision of a new heaven to dim. Disturb us, Lord, to dare more boldly, to venture on wilder seas where storms will show your mastery; where losing sight of land we shall find the stars. We ask you to push back the horizons of our hopes; and to push back the future in strength, courage, hope, and love. This we ask in the name of our Captain, who is Jesus Christ. Amen.

Prayer attributed to explorer Sir Francis Drake

DAY 3

Arrival in Saint-Jean-Pied-de-Port

I finally arrived in Madrid—safe, sound, and only slightly more jet-lagged than I'd like. From Madrid, I caught a flight to San Sebastián, Spain, then hopped in a cab crossing the French-Spanish border, and finally boarded a train in Bayonne, France, to Saint-Jean-Pied-de-Port, the starting point of my Camino.

Surprisingly, everything went smoothly. All the connections worked, and I arrived in Saint-Jean-Pied-de-Port even earlier than expected. On the train, I struck up a conversation with François, a kindhearted Canadian from Ottawa. We chatted for a while, and then we were joined by a father and son from Germany—Munich, to be exact. There's something strangely comforting about how quickly these fleeting relationships form among pilgrims.

François and I walked together to the Pilgrim Office to receive our credentials. As we neared the entrance, he was approached by a French-speaking traveler, and just like that, he was gone. No good-bye, no ceremony—just another soul swept up in the Camino's ever-shifting tide. I couldn't help but wonder if that moment was emblematic of this pilgrimage: encounters that are meaningful but momentary, with no expectation of permanence. I secured my customary scalloped shell and Pilgrim's *Credencial.* The Pilgrim's *Credencial* will be stamped along the way by the *albergues* (hostels) where I stay to verify that I've walked the Camino. In Santiago de Compostela, I will present it to receive my Pilgrim's *Certificado* (certification), granted to those who have walked at least one hundred kilometers of the Camino. The scalloped shell is the unofficial symbol of the Camino, and I will tie it to my backpack, indicating to others along the way that I am a pilgrim.

For a number of reasons, I have made the choice not to tell fellow pilgrims that I am an Episcopal priest. If I'm honest, I don't want to take any chance that I will fall into a default position of offering pastoral care because it is expected of me as a priest. I have come here to heal, to receive a measure of God's grace for myself. There were a couple of points during the day when I thought I might have to explain what I do for a living, but I managed to sidestep it—at least for today. It's funny how that can feel like both a relief and a missed opportunity.

Sitting at a sidewalk café in this quaint French village for dinner, I'm surrounded by people from all over the world. Yet, as I sit here in the midst of it all, I feel strangely alone. I'm sure some of it is the language barrier, and some of it is the exhaustion. Maybe part of the Camino is learning how to be alone—and discovering what's waiting in that space. To seek. To wait. To discover something. For now, I'll rest, pray, and prepare for the path ahead.

The Quiet Before the Climb

Now on that same day two [disciples] were going to a village called Emmaus, about seven miles from Jerusalem, and talking with each other about all these things that had happened. While they were talking and discussing, Jesus himself came near and went with them, but their eyes were kept from recognizing him. . . . As they came near the village to which they were going, [Jesus] walked ahead as if he were going on. But [the disciples] urged him strongly, saying, "Stay with us, because it is almost evening and the day is now nearly over." So he went in to stay with them. When he was at the table with them, he took bread, blessed and broke it, and gave it to them. Then their eyes were opened, and they recognized him; and he vanished from their sight.

—Luke 24:13–16, 28–31

Before they were called Christians, followers of Jesus were known simply as people of The Way. One of the most powerful post-resurrection appearances of Jesus takes place on the way to Emmaus, a village said to be seven miles from Jerusalem. Despite this striking detail in the Gospel narrative, Emmaus remains lost to us. Scholars have proposed roads and potential locations, but none have been definitively confirmed. Perhaps that's fitting. Maybe it's better this way—so that every town, even your town, can be Emmaus: a place where anyone might encounter the divine.

In Spanish, *Camino* means "path" or "way." It's the same word that gives us the title of the 2010 film *The Way*, starring Martin Sheen. The story follows a grieving father who embarks on the Camino de

Santiago after the death of his son. Like many others, I was deeply moved by this film, and eventually, I too chose to walk the Camino. I'm not sure I understood then what I now see clearly: that my journey on the Camino de Santiago echoed the story of the disciples on the road to Emmaus.

I find myself identifying with those grieving disciples. Their world had been shattered. The one they believed to be the Messiah had been crucified, and with him, their hope. Though reports circulated that the tomb was empty, and that some had even seen him alive, the disciples hadn't witnessed it themselves. They were confused, heartbroken, and lost. I know that feeling. At the start of my own journey, I wondered if my ministry was over—if my calling, once so clear, had been irreparably broken. I, too, felt disoriented and alone. Surrounded by cyclists, walkers, and diners, I was still isolated in my pain.

Even at this early stage of my pilgrimage—just like the disciples—I experienced moments of grace. On the Emmaus Road, it was in the breaking of bread that their eyes were opened, and they recognized Jesus. For me, it was a fleeting encounter with strangers on a train, the first of many seemingly small moments that would become sacred. Strangers became companions. Fleeting interactions revealed unexpected meaning. These encounters became sacraments—divine reminders that God meets us in our pain, our confusion, our questions.

I've often wondered, like so many others, why Jesus chose to remain hidden from the disciples until that moment at the table. Maybe it was so that the revelation would come not just from sight, but from something deeper—something that burned within them.

Sometimes it's not the sermon or the answer that reveals God, but the stillness, the walk, the meal, the unguarded conversation. On the Camino, I chose to keep my occupation a secret. Yet, through those anonymous interactions, God spoke—affirming my calling again and again, not through titles or recognition, but through presence and quiet grace.

In those moments, my heart burned—not from recognition of who I was to others but from rediscovery of who I truly am in the heart of God.

Reflection Questions:

1. Have you ever felt like the disciples on the road to Emmaus—confused, disoriented, or uncertain of where God was? What sustained you in that season?
2. Where in your life have seemingly small or fleeting moments become sacred—where God met you in quiet, unexpected ways?
3. Why do you think Jesus sometimes chooses to remain hidden until the "breaking of bread"? What might this say about how God reveals himself today?

Jesus, quiet companion on the road,
you draw near when we are uncertain,
when we feel alone even in a crowd,
when we step into something new and wonder if we belong.
You meet us in anonymous moments—
a stranger's kindness, a table shared,
a silence that begins to speak.
Give us courage to walk into unfamiliar spaces,
to embrace solitude without fear,
and to trust that not being seen doesn't mean we are unknown.
Let our hearts burn—not with certainty,
but with the quiet assurance that you are already with us,
in every conversation, every transition, every step.

Amen.

DAY 4

A Day I'll Never Forget

There's a good reason some pilgrims choose to start their Camino on the west side of the Pyrenees Mountains. Today was, without a doubt, the most physically demanding thing I've ever done. Fifteen miles of grueling ascent and descent—pure agony at times—but I made it. I began the day without breakfast (a mistake I won't repeat), and the first five miles nearly broke me. The total ascent to the peak of the Pyrenees at 4,141 feet, in the rain, was relentless. Every step felt like a negotiation with my body. By God's grace, there was a man with a travel trailer along the path selling *café con leche*, fruit, and snacks.

I stopped at Orisson for breakfast and was greeted by some company—two Finnish women, one of whom was actively shedding weight from her overpacked backpack, a common mistake of first-time pilgrims. It was both hilarious and oddly profound, a living metaphor for the Camino itself: the shedding of unnecessary burdens, both physical and spiritual. For a long time, I debated whether to stop and stay the night at Orisson. It's a common choice for many, given the difficulty of the climb from Saint-Jean-Pied-de-Port to Roncesvalles—widely considered the toughest stretch of the entire pilgrimage. After losing a day due to my flight delay, however, I felt compelled to press on. I'm so glad I did.

The rain began not long after I left Orisson and barely let up the rest of the day. I walked mostly alone through the steady downpour, soaked to the bone, with fog clinging to the mountains like a second skin. When my heart raced from the strain of the climb, I'd stop to catch my breath and let my pulse slow. Those frequent pauses, which at first frustrated me, soon became sacred spaces. Somewhere along the way, in that wet and weary solitude, prayer took over. Rather than grow discouraged by my lack of progress, I began using that time to pray—interceding for my family, my staff, my church, and my friends. I had a particularly emotional moment praying for my daughter Kristel and her husband—tears streaming down my face in a way I couldn't stop or explain. It felt like a return to the very core of my vocation. This mountain, this silence, this suffering, all brought me back to the heart of who I am.

Along the path, I met a cheerful Spanish group and took a few photos with them—moments of warmth amid the cold. Earlier in the journey, I connected with two wonderful Brits—Adam and Joanne. Adam walked with me for a bit as Joanne motored ahead. Finally, frustrated with our slower pace, Joanne, waiting ahead, told Adam they needed to walk faster if they were going to meet their goal for the day. Just that short time walking with Adam, diverting my mind from the difficulty of the climb, felt like a gift. Younger and fitter than me, they move at a faster pace, so I may not see them again, but our short time together brought real joy. Despite the misery of the weather and the exhaustion in my bones, I kept hearing in my spirit: The joy of the Lord is my strength. Somehow, even as I labored up steep paths and slipped down muddy trails, that joy carried me.

Tomorrow promises an easier day. Tonight, I'm grateful for Advil, dry clothes, a cold beer, and the peace of having made it through. Thank you, Jesus—for the mountain, the rain, the solitude, and the grace to walk through it all.

Strength Found in Surrender

Have you not known? Have you not heard? The LORD is the everlasting God, the Creator of the ends of the earth. He does not faint or grow weary; his understanding is unsearchable. He gives power to the faint, and strengthens the powerless. Even youths will faint and be weary, and the young will fall exhausted; but those who wait for the Lord shall renew their strength, they shall mount up with wings like eagles, they shall run and not be weary, they shall walk and not faint.

—Isaiah 40:28–31

Revisiting this day in my journal brings back a flood of memories—both joyful and painful. What stands out most is a deepening awareness that the spiritual journey involves both activity and rest. *The Rule of St. Benedict* speaks of this balance: the active life and the contemplative life. For me—and likely for many in the Western world—the active life comes more naturally. Stillness, reflection, and rest, on the other hand, often feel elusive or even indulgent.

With the ambitious goal of walking five hundred miles in about a month, the active life was not only assumed on the Camino—it was expected, even praised. Rest was the last thing on my mind. Yet, God knew what I truly needed. This is the God who rested on the seventh day and commanded his people to do likewise. So, on this first day of walking, I found myself unexpectedly at rest—not by choice, but by necessity. The question became: What would I do with this forced rest?

When I began the Camino, I was carrying an extra sixty pounds and a backpack of twenty-five pounds, a weight that made every incline a battle. During the grueling ascent, I seriously considered turning back. In the stillness that came with necessary pauses, my first thoughts were harsh and condemning. I berated myself for being out of shape, for the professional conflict that had brought me here, and for what felt like yet another failure. The physical rest I so badly needed turned out to be just as painful emotionally. My body ached, but so did my heart.

As rain poured and my body throbbed, I found myself crying out to God—for relief, for help, for anything. Time and again in the Old Testament, God's people cry out for justice, for mercy, and God hears. In Exodus, we're reminded that God heard the cries of his people in bondage and delivered them. There I was, on a mountainside in Spain, wondering: Would God hear me?

My cries were full of frustration and anger, mostly directed at myself. In complete exhaustion, I repeated the same desperate plea to God, waiting for a response. Then, quietly, it came: "Talk to me. Pray for others." So that's what I did. When my legs or lungs could go no further, I stopped, quieted my heart, and listened. I waited for God to bring someone to mind—and then prayed. If I was stymied as to what to pray for them, I would simply pray, "God, show up for them as you are for me." In that waiting, my strength returned. Somehow, I found the energy to keep walking. God had heard me, and in turning my focus outward, I found renewal. I found grace.

Reflection Questions:

1. Where in your life do you feel weary right now—physically, emotionally, or spiritually? How might God be inviting you to rest, even if it feels unproductive?
2. Have you ever found your inner critic loudest during times of stillness? What helps you shift from self-condemnation to self-compassion?
3. Who might God be bringing to your mind to pray for in your own moments of waiting or weakness? How could praying for others be a pathway to your own renewal?

God of the weary and the worn, when the climb is steep
and the path is soaked in sorrow,
teach us to pause—not in defeat, but in trust.
In our exhaustion, meet us.
In our frustration, speak to us.
When we feel like turning back,
remind us that strength often begins in surrender.
Turn our prayers outward,
that even in our struggle, we may lift others up.
And when we cannot go further,
give us the grace to wait—and find you waiting with us.

Amen.

DAY 5

The Camino Continues

A Day of Progress

Today was easier than yesterday, though still challenging. My body is starting to adjust to the demands of walking fifteen-mile days—well, today it was actually nineteen miles. It's a bit more manageable now, but the fatigue is still there. As expected, there were more people on the trail today, but I still found moments of solitude. There's something to be treasured in those quiet moments, walking alone with only the sound of my footsteps and the occasional greeting from another pilgrim.

Last night's hostel in Roncesvalles was a real treat, everything I needed and more. Tonight's accommodations in Larrasoaña are a different experience. I'm sharing a room with two men and one woman, which isn't unusual, but what really stands out is the shared shower facilities. There are separate stalls, but the area is communal. It's an interesting aspect of the Camino's blend of personal space and shared experiences. I had dinner with my British friends, Adam and Joanne. Unfortunately, Adam is struggling with some serious blisters. He didn't break in his boots properly before starting, and without sock liners, the blisters have taken a heavy toll. They've decided to skip the leg to Pamplona and take a bus to get medical care, hoping to heal up so they can continue their journey.

When Solitude Welcomes the Sacred

Jacob was left alone; and a man wrestled with him until daybreak. When the man saw that he did not prevail against Jacob, he struck him on the hip socket; and Jacob's hip was put out of joint as he wrestled with him. Then he said, "Let me go, for the day is breaking." But Jacob said, "I will not let you go, unless you bless me." So he said to him, "What is your name?" And he said, "Jacob." Then the man said, "You shall no longer be called Jacob, but Israel, for you have striven with God and with humans, and have prevailed."

—Genesis 32:24–28

This scripture is one of my favorite Bible stories. Jacob is returning home after having been on the run from his brother Esau, whom Jacob had cheated out of both his birthright and blessing. Jacob isn't sure how he'll be received back home. He sends his family ahead while he remains behind on the banks of the river, weighing the consequences of returning home. In the text above, Jacob is wrestling with an angel of the Lord.

What fascinates me about this passage is the message that, ultimately, to be blessed, Jacob must let go. He must decide whether to cling to what he already has or release it in hopes of receiving something greater.

Though it was only the second day of walking the Camino, a recurring tension between solitude and community was already emerging. As an extrovert, community comes naturally to me. Honestly, I've never valued—or even desired—the practice of solitude. Growing up in the Baptist church, I struggled with the expected "quiet time" with the Lord. It just wasn't how I was wired.

On my first day of walking, solitude felt heavy. The silence exposed my fears, regrets, and self-judgment. Without the distraction of conversation or activity, I was left alone with my thoughts—and that was something I didn't want to face. Solitude felt like isolation, a stark reminder of my limits and shortcomings.

The rain made it impossible to see more than a few feet ahead. This blanket of rain seemed to amplify the isolation I felt. Henri Nouwen writes, "To live a spiritual life we must first find the courage to enter into the desert of our loneliness and to change it by gentle and persistent efforts into a garden of solitude. . . . The movement from loneliness to solitude, however, is the beginning of any spiritual life because it is the movement from the restless senses to the restful spirit, from the outward-reaching cravings to the inward-reaching search, from the fearful clinging to the fearless play."[1] The first day on the Camino, I couldn't let go of the struggle long enough to experience the beauty of solitude.

On the second day, something changed. As I walked the long miles, my body began to adjust—and strangely, so did my spirit. The same quiet that initially felt oppressive now offered peace. The

1. Henri J. M. Nouwen, *Reaching Out: The Three Movements of the Spiritual Life* (Doubleday, 1975), 23.

rhythm of my footsteps became a kind of prayer. The occasional greeting from a fellow pilgrim interrupted my solitude but didn't disturb it. It became a gentle sign of the community that would be there for me at the end of my day.

My conversation with God the day before, which felt forced by exhaustion and desperation, came naturally on this day. I began to see that solitude isn't the absence of connection, it's the space where deeper connection becomes possible. In solitude, I wasn't alone. I was present—with myself, with God, and with the subtle beauty of the journey around me.

Reflection Questions:

1. What struggles—internal or external—are you currently wrestling with, and what might God be inviting you to release?

2. When have you mistaken solitude for loneliness? What helped shift that perspective?

3. Where do you see "God's handwriting" in your ordinary, daily journey?

O God who walks with the wanderer,
In this silence, I feel alone,
wrestling with my fears and doubts.
But like Jacob, I will not let go—
not until you bless me.
Transform this struggle, Lord,
and rename me with your grace.
May this solitude deepen my faith,
and may I walk forward,
challenged but stronger in you.
In the name of Christ,

Amen.

DAY 6

From the Penthouse to the Outhouse

I survived another day on the Camino—thirty kilometers today, about nineteen miles. The terrain wasn't as steep as yesterday, which was a welcome relief, but my body is still reeling from fifteen miles of wind and rain two days ago. Honestly, I feel like I've gone fifteen rounds in a prize fight. Every muscle aches, every joint complains, but somehow, I'm still moving forward.

Despite the physical toll, the journey continues to be an incredible experience. I've met people from all over the world—so many different backgrounds and stories. One of the most perplexing things to me is how few are here for religious reasons. It feels strangely antithetical to the idea of pilgrimage, and yet, maybe God has brought them here for reasons even they can't see yet. Perhaps that's true for me too.

Today's walk was mostly flat, which was a blessing. Somewhere outside Pamplona, I came across a small chapel in Trinidad de Arre where I stepped inside and said a few quiet prayers. There was a sense of divine presence in that little space—simple, sacred. It stayed with me.

Tonight, I'm staying in Cizur Menor. I shared a meal with a delightful couple from the Netherlands—Harry and Josie. If I were guessing,

I would say they were in their late sixties or early seventies. I'm discovering that the Camino has no age barriers; it is walked by both young and old. They've been walking from their home, each pulling a two-wheeled cart with their bags strapped on top. They'd already walked 2,750 kilometers (1,708 miles) by the time they arrived in Saint-Jean-Pied-de-Port—where I started. Their endurance, their spirit, was inspiring.

On the Camino there are three types of albergues that range from simplicity to luxury. Of course, the word *luxury* is a relative term when talking about Camino accommodations. The simplest and therefore least expensive are the albergues hosted by Roman Catholic churches. While it is the least expensive, that doesn't mean trashy; it just means fewer bells and whistles. The next step up in accommodation and cost are municipal albergues operated by the city in which they are located. The most expensive and luxurious are the private albergues. Of course, there is also the most luxurious accommodation possible, a private room and shower in a hotel.

The meal was delightful, but let's just say the accommodation has taken a sharp turn downward. Last night, I was in a beautiful hostel where a kind *hospitalero* washed our clothes for a small fee—practically a luxury. Tonight, I've gone from the penthouse to the outhouse. I'm sharing a small room with five other pilgrims, one of whom is a woman. For a modest American, it makes even simple things like changing clothes a bit of a logistical challenge. The coed bathrooms—with separate shower stalls but shared space—still catch me off guard. We're not in Kansas anymore, Toto.

To top it off, I had the worst night's sleep I've had on this journey. A very large man traveling with his daughter was in our room, and his snoring was epic. Think of a freight train through a tunnel. In spite of the physical discomfort, I still love the walk. Because I'm slower than most—a drag on the friends I've made so far—I spend much of the day alone. Strangely, for someone as extroverted as I am, I've come to treasure that solitude. I had forgotten how to talk with God like this. There's something deeply joyful about remembering and returning to that quiet communion.

The Sacred Hidden in the Ordinary

Do nothing from selfish ambition or conceit, but in humility regard others as better than yourselves. Let each of you look not to your own interests, but to the interests of others. Let the same mind be in you that was in Christ Jesus, who, though he was in the form of God, did not regard equality with God as something to be exploited, but emptied himself, taking the form of a slave, being born in human likeness. And being found in human form, he humbled himself and became obedient to the point of death—even death on a cross.

—Philippians 2:3–8

The Episcopal tradition is, like its Roman Catholic parent, a sacramental church. In our catechism, a sacrament is defined as "an outward and visible sign of an inward and spiritual grace." More importantly, sacramental theology finds the presence of God—the divine—in the ordinary things of life. This presence of God in the everyday is one of the beauties of the Christian message. It is revealed in the incarnation of God, who became flesh and was born not in a palace, but in a stable, and laid in a manger—a feed trough.

The biblical passage above, considered by some New Testament scholars to be an ancient Christian hymn, encapsulates this truth, telling us that Jesus humbled himself. It's interesting to note that the etymology of the word *humbled*, used to describe Jesus, comes from the Latin word *humus*, meaning "earth." You can't get more ordinary than dirt. In God's hands, even the most ordinary thing can become holy, extraordinary.

As I walked the Camino on this day, the sacred surfaced not in the grand church of Pamplona, but in a small chapel just outside the city. It's not that the cathedral in Pamplona isn't sacred, but it was while saying prayers in this humble, out-of-the-way chapel that I experienced the presence of God. I often tell my parishioners that their church isn't sacred because it's a church building, but because of the holy things that happen within it—baptisms, weddings, funerals, confessions, healings, and worship.

As I sat there in silence, saying my prayers, I was struck by the awareness that I was only one of thousands—perhaps millions—of pilgrims who had offered prayers in that holy space. It might even be possible that thousands, even millions more, will do the same after me. I am but one thread in a tapestry of prayers—God using countless ordinary people to weave something sacred. That place is made holy because holy people have done holy things there on their journeys. What I was doing that day was helping to preserve that holiness, so that other pilgrims might one day experience the same peace I was experiencing.

Then, as if God hadn't already been so good to me, I found God's presence once again in the ordinary act of sharing a meal with Harry and Josie. Is it any wonder we so often find Jesus eating with others in the Gospels? Jesus takes bread and wine and makes them his body and blood. The ordinary, in God's hands, becomes holy. In God's hands, *we* become holy.

Reflection Questions:

1. How does Christ's humility—his willingness to "empty himself"—challenge the way you approach others?
2. Who are the people in your life whose quiet faithfulness has helped weave the sacred tapestry you now stand within?
3. What might it mean for you to be a "keeper of holy ground" for others?

God of the everyday,
teach me to recognize your presence
not only in sacred spaces,
but in the ordinary moments I often overlook.
When beauty feels distant
and discomfort clouds my spirit,
remind me that you are just as near
in quiet prayers and shared meals
as in cathedrals and grand gestures.
Help me return to the joy of stillness,
to the grace of simple presence,
and to the truth that nothing is too common
to be made holy by your love.

Amen.

DAY 7

Grace and Peace from the Road

Every day feels like a gift, even when it's difficult. In the evenings, when we gather for meals with a glass of wine and stories from the road, the Camino somehow feels smaller and bigger at the same time. Last night, my tablemates were from the Netherlands, Brazil, and Spain. The conversations, the laughter, the diversity—it's just incredible. Today I walked for a while with a woman from Hungary, another beautiful soul among so many I've met along the way.

The walk itself was gentle—my fourth day of walking, and thankfully one of the easier ones. Not flat but not punishing either. Just enough elevation to remind me I wasn't strolling the Boorman Trail back home in Texas. Toward the end, my right knee started to ache on the downhill stretches. I've discovered the hard way that there are two essentials on the Camino: earplugs and hiking poles. The heat today didn't help either—about 30 degrees Celsius, which is 86 degrees Fahrenheit. Not unbearable, but relentless. The showers continue to be a bit of a saga. Tonight's wasn't coed—thankfully—but I nearly slipped and fell while getting in. That would've been a dramatic way to end my Camino.

I tried to take a detour to a spectacular church in Eunate just outside Puente la Reina, but I couldn't find it. I'm learning to let those missed turns go—they're part of the pilgrimage too.

What really stood out to me today was a gathering of pilgrims at the iron sculpture at the peak of the Alto del Perdón. There's something powerful about that place—pilgrims pausing at the summit, together and yet alone in their own journeys.

I'm staying in a wonderful hostel tonight, complete with washers, dryers, and a buffet dinner. We were even treated to traditional Basque music before the meal. These little gifts—unexpected music, shared laughter, clean clothes—feel like gifts from God in a way I didn't anticipate.

As always, I hold everyone back home in my prayers. The solitude of walking creates such sacred space. Without the busyness of everyday life, there's room—room for silence, for prayer, for listening. I, in turn, feel the prayers offered by those praying for me back home, and I'm so grateful for them.

When Many Nations Worship One God

Nations shall come to your light, and kings to the brightness of your dawn. Lift up your eyes and look around; they all gather together, they come to you; your sons shall come from far away, and your daughters shall be carried on their nurses' arms. Then you shall see and be radiant; your heart shall thrill and rejoice, because the abundance of the sea shall be brought to you, the wealth of the nations shall come to you. . . . Your gates shall always be open; day and night they shall not be shut, will never be shut . . . they shall call you the City of the LORD, *the Zion of the Holy One of Israel.*

—Isaiah 60:3–5, 11, 14

It's so easy to assume that our way of seeing the world is the only way. That our theology is the only correct theology. That our style of worship is the only legitimate form. That our political views are the only defensible ones. That our ethical framework is the only proper way to live. This narrowness, I think, is a particular danger for Americans. We live in a vast country where cultural diversity exists, but exposure to it is often a choice—something we can engage with or ignore.

Being confronted with other cultures—or even subcultures—has a way of breaking that illusion. It forces us to recognize that other valid viewpoints exist. That feeling was intensified on the Camino. The previous evening, I sat at a table with people from the Netherlands, Brazil, Spain, and the United States. The next day, I stood atop the Alto del Perdón, surrounded by the sound of countless languages rising together in reverent noise. That night, I shared dinner and Indigenous Basque music with Nicole, a police officer from Germany. It was a small foretaste of the day the prophet Isaiah envisions: "Nations shall come to your light, and kings to the brightness of your dawn."

These moments, when we encounter a world far larger than our own, are sacred reminders not to limit God. Saint Paul reminds us that "For now we see in a mirror, dimly, but then we will see face to face. Now I know only in part; then I will know fully, even as I have been fully known" (1 Corinthians 13:12). And there's a saying—humorous but true—that God created us in his image, and we've been trying to return the favor ever since. Avoiding this temptation to create God in our image will keep us ever open to the new and wonderful things God wants to do in our lives.

Listening—truly listening—is one of the most important spiritual disciplines. It's how we begin to grasp that others have lived different lives, carry different wounds, and have encountered God in ways we haven't. When we listen to others and to our own hearts, we begin to hear God more clearly. Then, together, we can return to Scripture—not to prove a point, but to discover how our stories fit into God's greater story. Above all, we must learn to listen: to others, to our hearts, and to God.

Reflection Questions:

1. When have you experienced the presence of God through a culture, language, or tradition different from your own?
2. Are there ways you have unknowingly tried to limit God by confining him to your own worldview or tradition?
3. How can you cultivate a deeper habit of listening to others, to your own inner life, and to God?

God of the road and the resting place,
thank you for the gift of each day—
thank you for laughter shared around simple meals,
for strangers who become companions.
Forgive me when I assume my view is the only one,
my path the only path, my faith the full picture.
Help me to listen—really listen—to the stories of others,
to the silence within, and to your Spirit moving in it all.
Let every step teach me more about humility,
every detour remind me that grace walks with me,
and every face reflect a piece of your image.
May I never be afraid of mystery.
May I never grow too proud to learn.
And may the light of your glory
draw all nations, all voices, all hearts
into your great and beautiful story.

Amen.

DAY 8

No Room at the Inn

What a day. I walked twenty and a half miles—my longest stretch so far—only to arrive in Villamayor de Monjardín and find that there was no room left at the albergue. After that many miles, the words "no beds available" hit a little harder than usual. In true Camino fashion, grace arrived in the form of a fellow pilgrim. Julia from Houston, who had arrived early enough to find a bed in the albergue, offered me her air mattress. So tonight, I'm sleeping in an open-air handball court with a metal roof overhead on Julia's air mattress. It's not glamorous, but somehow it feels like exactly where I'm supposed to be. A reminder of Jesus' birth narrative found in the Gospel of Luke, where there was "no room at the inn"—and a reminder that hospitality on this journey comes in many forms.

Earlier in the day, I had a small but meaningful goodbye. Peter and Michael, friends from England whom I've been walking with, ended their Camino today. They were only walking for a week before returning home, and while we hadn't traveled together long, it was still hard to see them go. Many Europeans, due to the proximity of the Camino to their homes, have the option of walking only a portion of the Camino and then returning to pick up where they left off the previous year. I've started taking pictures of the people I meet—pilgrims who become friends, then disappear like waves receding from the shore. These goodbyes are beginning to shape the rhythm of the journey.

There was a moment of unexpected delight this afternoon when we passed through Ayegui. In this town, a former monastery, now occupied by Bodegas de Irache, has a fountain on an exterior wall with dual spigots dispensing both wine and water. Yes—wine. Yes, of course I partook. It is a tradition to drink from the fountain using the scalloped shell given to pilgrims at the beginning of their Camino. A small sip, a brief pause, a shared smile with other pilgrims. One of those moments that makes the Camino feel both ancient and alive.

Where There's No Room, There's Still Grace

In those days a decree went out from Emperor Augustus that all the world should be registered. This was the first registration and was taken while Quirinius was governor of Syria. All went to their own towns to be registered. Joseph also went from the town of Nazareth in Galilee to Judea, to the city of David called Bethlehem, because he was descended from the house and family of David. He went to be registered with Mary, to whom he was engaged and who was expecting a child. While they were there, the time came for her to deliver her child. And she gave birth to her firstborn son and wrapped him in bands of cloth, and laid him in a manger, because there was no place for them in the inn.

—Luke 2:1–7

One of the challenges of reading Scripture two thousand years after it was written is the temptation to overlay our modern cultural assumptions onto the text. Such is the case with the familiar birth narrative of Jesus found in the Gospel of Luke. Since the time of King James I of England and the first authorized translation of the Bible into English, we've been told that there was no room in the inn for Mary and Joseph when they arrived in Bethlehem. Even many modern translations continue to render the Greek word *katalyma* as "inn."

However, more accurate and recent translations interpret katalyma as "guest room." This distinction matters. First, it's unlikely that Joseph, returning to his ancestral home, would have had no relatives to stay with. This wasn't a world of Holiday Inns and Marriotts—it was the ancient Middle East, where hospitality was not just expected but required. In Jewish culture, welcoming the traveler was a sacred duty. Hosts were expected to offer lodging—typically up to three nights—without question.

So, a more faithful reading of katalyma suggests that the guest room in the family home was already full, likely due to the influx of visitors arriving for the census. As a result, Mary and Joseph were offered space in the part of the house where animals were kept—a stable of sorts. This "stable" was not a detached barn, but typically a lower room attached to the house, where a manger—essentially a feeding trough—was available for the baby Jesus.

What matters most for our reflection is this: Hospitality has always been a core value in the Jewish tradition, and it continued as a defining mark of the Christian faith. Saint Benedict, in his Rule for monastic life, instructed monks to welcome every guest as if they were receiving Christ himself.[2] How fitting then, that along the Camino de

---

2. Timothy Fry, ed., *The Rule of St. Benedict in English* (Liturgical Press, 1982), 73.

Santiago, Bodegas de Irache uses the site of a former monastery to offer fountains that pour not only water, but wine, for the refreshment of weary pilgrims.

Hospitality became one of the dominant themes of my Camino pilgrimage. I learned this vividly on a night when there was no room left in the albergue. I was tired and unsure where I'd sleep—until Julia offered me her air mattress. It was a small gesture, but one that made my night tangibly better. In that moment, I was reminded that God is a God of provision—known in the Old Testament as *YHWH-Yireh*, "The Lord Will Provide."

What I also learned that night, however, is that God's provision is not always predictable or luxurious. God provides what we need, not necessarily what we want. If the King of the universe could be born in a stable and be laid in a manger, I could sleep on a cold handball court. The community that formed around me—Mary, Maura, Scott, and Kim, all sleeping nearby—was not forged through shared comfort, but through shared sacrifice and unexpected grace.

Reflection Questions:

1. Are there moments in your life where you've been told, in one way or another, "there's no room"? What did you learn through that experience—about yourself, others, or God?
2. Think about the people who've come and gone in your life. What do their departures teach you about impermanence, gratitude, and how to hold relationships loosely yet meaningfully?
3. Where might God be inviting you to offer simple, sacrificial hospitality—something small that could make a big difference in someone else's life?

Lord Jesus,
you entered this world with no place to lay your head,
yet you were never without the shelter of the Father's love.
When doors are closed and comfort is scarce,
remind me that your presence is enough.
Teach me to trust in your provision,
even when it comes in humble, unexpected ways.
Make my heart a place where you are always welcome,
and help me offer that same welcome to others.

Amen.

DAY 9

The Longest Day

Last night was horrific. I might have slept for two hours at most, and then I was back on my feet for another thirty-one kilometers—almost twenty miles. The walk felt endless. Every step tested my body and spirit in ways I didn't expect. The trail stretched on and on, and for a good part of the day, I was convinced I had finally achieved what I thought I wanted: isolation. I had completely separated myself from the friends I'd made along the way. Solitude, in all its fullness.

And yet, just as I was writing these words—feeling alone, tired, and perhaps indulging in a little self-pity, my Camino buddies turned the corner and found me. I genuinely didn't expect to see them again. There's a lesson in that, I think. Even when you believe you're walking alone, community has a way of returning, often when you need it most.

With all that time alone today, I had space to reflect deeply. One thing that struck me was how radically different the world feels when experienced on foot. Moving slowly, step by step, allows your mind to open, your heart to notice. I could so clearly imagine Jesus walking with his disciples, teaching as they wandered dusty paths. When he spoke in parables—so many rooted in agriculture—I can see him pausing, gesturing to the fields around him and saying: "See the field of wheat and the tares that grow in its midst . . ." The land itself became his canvas.

I've also been overwhelmed by the quiet kindness of others. There's something deeply moving about the generosity that surfaces out here. When kindness is extended by those who aren't people of faith, it causes me to pause and ask: What difference does our faith really make in a world like this? Surely it must be more than good deeds or clever theology.

Today, I think I found part of the answer: eschatology. That is, the hope of what's to come. Many people believe the world is on a steady path of progress, that things are slowly improving. I think, however, that without a true understanding of humanity's brokenness, that belief is naive. Buddhism emphasizes detachment from suffering. Hinduism offers the progressive enlightenment of reincarnation. It's the Judeo-Christian story that strikes me as both the most realistic and the most hopeful: This world is broken, yes, but God will one day make it right. The mighty will be brought down from their thrones, and the lowly will be lifted up. This vision of an alternate community—a kingdom not of this world—was planted in me long ago. It's never really left. Church, at its best, is a people who believe in that vision and act on it.

Near the end of the walk today, I noticed something else: When I can see my destination, when I can fix my eyes on where I'm going, the walk feels easier. There's power in having a visible goal. As I saw the city of Los Arcos rising in the distance, something inside me lifted. My heart quickened. Hope returned. *Dear God, lay before me your vision for my life that I might continually strive for its fulfillment.*

Hurry Is the Enemy of Love

Then the righteous will answer him, "Lord, when was it that we saw you hungry and gave you food, or thirsty and gave you something to drink? And when was it that we saw you a stranger and welcomed you, or naked and gave you clothing? And when was it that we saw you sick or in prison and visited you?" And the king will answer them, "Truly I tell you, just as you did it to one of the least of these who are members of my family, you did it to me."

—Matthew 25:37–40

In our fast-paced world, speed is often praised as a virtue. We rush through our mornings, our meetings, our meals—and if we're not careful, we begin to rush through life itself. When we slow down, we realize something profound: The pace of love is slow. Psychiatrist Carl Jung once remarked, "Hurry is not *of* the Devil; it *is* the Devil."[3] It's not just that hurry distracts us from God—it becomes a barrier to grace itself. When we hurry, we miss the sacred in the ordinary. We fail to see the image of God in the stranger, those who walk beside us.

We overlook the sheep that belong to Jesus—those who don't look like us, think like us, or even believe like us. Jesus once said, "I have other sheep that do not belong to this fold. I must bring them also, and

3. Richard J. Foster, *Celebration of Discipline: The Path to Spiritual Growth* (Harper Collins, 1978), 15.

they will listen to my voice. So there will be one flock, one shepherd" (John 10:16). This challenges our narrow categories. Who are these "other sheep"? People overlooked by our religiosity and ignored in our hurry.

Reading my journal entry written on this day, I cringed a bit. When talking of other religions, I found it necessary to assert the superiority of Christianity. Don't get me wrong, I believe with all my heart that the Christian story, the story of Jesus, is the truest story about God's love for us. However, God doesn't need me to defend him. As my seminary professor said to me once, "God is big enough to weed his own garden." Jesus tells us exactly how judgment will come—not based on doctrine or status, but on what we do for "the least of these" (Matthew 25:31–46). The hungry, the stranger, the sick, the prisoner. The people we're most likely to overlook when we're in a rush.

Slowing down is not just good for our souls—it's essential to living like Jesus. We can't love our neighbor at full speed. We can't recognize the face of Christ in the least of these if we never stop long enough to look. When we slow our steps, we begin to see again. The person begging outside the store becomes more than an inconvenience. The lonely friend becomes more than a phone call we've been meaning to return. The world around us begins to shine with God's presence.

Jesus walked everywhere he went. He was often interrupted—but never rushed. His pace left room for compassion. He saw Zacchaeus in the tree. He stopped for blind Bartimaeus. He noticed the woman who touched the hem of his robe. He paused long enough to wash his disciples' feet. What about us? We miss these holy interruptions when we live in a constant state of hurry. Today, pause. Breathe. Listen. Take the slower road. Choose mercy over movement. Because in the end, we will not be asked how fast we lived, but how well we loved.

Reflection Questions:

1. What in your life is pushing you to live in a state of hurry?
2. Who might you be overlooking in your rush?
3. How can you create space today to notice and serve "the least of these"?

Lord, teach me to walk at your pace—unhurried,
attentive, open.
When the road feels long and I am weary,
remind me that I am never truly alone.
Help me see those I overlook in my hurry.
Open my eyes to the face of Christ in the least of these.
Guard me from pride, from the need to be right,
and guide me instead toward mercy and compassion.
Fix my eyes on your Kingdom.
Give me strength for each step
and hope that lifts when the end comes into view.

Amen.

DAY 10

From Viana to Logroño and Beyond

A quick update as I prepare to leave Viana. For the first time in three nights, I actually slept well—deep, uninterrupted sleep. It's amazing what a good night's rest can do for the soul. Yesterday, we walked another twenty miles and arrived in Viana, just east of Logroño. Tapas with friends from California and Virginia turned into a cultural adventure with anchovies and mushrooms. Honestly, not my favorite, but when in Spain! Fully rested, I can manage the walk in stride. Just ten kilometers to Logroño, where there's a festival: free beer and fish, or so I've heard.

This morning, the knees feel good, no blisters—thank you, Jesus. I found myself thinking: I feel like Forrest Gump. "I just started walking." Once again, I'm struck by how different life looks when you're walking instead of driving. The world slows down. You start to notice the beauty of an olive orchard, a vineyard glistening in the morning sun, or a stranger's kindness at a water fountain. As I walk in solitude, I am reminded that I've lost track of Adam and Joanne over the past few days; they've had to slow down a bit. I trust and hope we'll reconnect.

There was a celebration today in Logroño—the anniversary of the independence of the state of Rioja. Grandparents, parents, children—all dressed in traditional costumes, parading through the streets. I even got to see a reenactment of the battle that won their freedom. It was a beautiful surprise, even though the promised fish never materialized. I did, however, eat a delicious Spanish tortilla. So, reenergized by a delicious meal, I walked on, away from the crowds, carrying the memory of the music, the laughter, the smells of grilled food and dusty wine, toward a quieter tomorrow. My body is sore, my spirit is light, and the road ahead calls.

I left the usual group of American pilgrims behind in Logroño to get a head start for a lighter day tomorrow when we plan to meet in Nájera for the Italy-Spain soccer game with some Italian friends.

Then, as I rounded a corner after dinner and conversation in Navarrete, who should appear but Adam and Joanne. They walked thirty-four kilometers today just to catch up. Adam's blisters are healing, and I told him that half of the United States had been praying for him. It's strange how fast relationships form on the Camino, and how deeply they matter. Seeing them again felt like reuniting with family. It gave me a glimpse of something eternal—a small window into the joy of being reunited one day with those we've loved and lost. I often preach about that joy at funerals, and tonight, I caught a foretaste of it.

When Friendship Is the Gift

Two are better than one, because they have a good reward for their toil. For if they fall, one will lift up the other; but woe to one who is alone and falls and does not have another to help. Again, if two lie together, they keep warm; but how can one keep warm alone? And though one might prevail against another, two will withstand one. A threefold cord is not quickly broken.

—Ecclesiastes 4:9–12

One of the most profound lessons the Camino taught me was about the nature of friendship—how it can be deeply rooted, yet also transient, and that both forms are equally holy. The people I met along the journey—some of whom I may never see again—shaped me in ways I couldn't fully grasp at the time. There was a sacredness to those encounters, a profound connection that transcended the fleeting nature of our time together. Even now, I carry with me their stories, their laughter, and the way they shared their journey with me, without the need to hold on to them.

The transitory nature of some friendships is, in fact, part of their beauty. I've come to understand that not every connection is meant to endure. Some are gifts that arrive in the moment, brief as the wind, leaving behind the scent of grace, a reminder that we are never truly alone, even when the road feels solitary. In many ways, I believe that God brings certain people into our lives for a season, to teach us about his love, his presence in the ordinary, and the way God's grace shows up in the most unexpected forms.

It's remarkable how the Camino forces us to confront the tension between the temporary and the permanent. Yet both are essential to the journey. The fleeting friendships teach us to love without clinging, to value each moment without the need to hold on to it forever. The lasting relationships, those that endure, remind us of the deep beauty of community—that we are not meant to walk this road alone, but to support one another through all of life's highs and lows.

The thing is, in the moment, we can never know for sure which friendships are temporary and which ones will last. This is why it's so important to give each friendship our all. Joanne and I are still connected via the internet, but I haven't heard from Adam since the days of the Camino. Yet, I know that the bond I shared with him, however brief, was significant. He was there for me during those early days of the pilgrimage when I struggled with exhaustion and doubts as to whether I could complete the journey. He and Joanne broke bread with me when I felt entirely alone, offering not just company but a reminder that I wasn't walking this road in isolation.

The real spiritual growth on the Camino didn't come from the distance I covered or the places I saw. It came from the people I met, the ones who walked beside me for only a short time, and those who continue to journey with me. All of them were God's gifts to me, teaching me that love can be both eternal and fleeting, and that each connection holds something sacred.

Reflection Questions:

1. What does it mean to love deeply without clinging, and how can you apply this in your current relationships?

2. In what ways do you experience God's presence in your encounters with others, both familiar and unfamiliar?

3. What does it look like for you to invite God into every connection you make?

Lord, thank you for the friendships that have shaped my journey—those that have lasted and those that were for a season. Help me to love deeply, without clinging, and to embrace the sacredness of every encounter. Teach me to cherish the fleeting and the eternal, knowing that you are with me in every moment.

Amen.

DAY 11

When the Quiet Speaks

Today was a short walking day, for which my feet were more than grateful. I had breakfast and then walked with Adam and Joanne as far as Nájera. We parted ways again for now, but sharing the road with them, even briefly, was comforting. I fell into a fortunate situation upon arriving, finding a bed in a newer albergue with really lovely facilities. Of course, privacy remains a rare luxury on the Camino, but this place surprised me with clever cubby spaces for my belongings. It's funny how small comforts like that begin to feel like extravagance out here.

Later, I had dinner with Mona from the Netherlands and Andreas from Italy, and we watched the Spain-Italy game together. European Cup fever is in the air—flags waving, cheers erupting in the streets. It was a nice way to end the day, even if I didn't have the same group around me as before. If I'm honest, today was also a day of inner struggle. I've started to sense this might be the beginning of the end of pushing long distances in an effort to stay with certain people. I may start walking more independently now, letting the path decide who I end up beside. As beautiful as these connections are, there's something calling me into solitude as well.

And in the quiet of today's shorter walk, I found myself wrestling with something deeper. A heaviness settled in—not about the journey, not about the aches and blisters, but about my vocation. I love being a priest. I can't imagine not being one, but I've been struggling with my current role. There's a kind of weariness that doesn't come from walking twenty miles—it comes from carrying questions you don't know how to answer. I love almost everything else about my life, but today, I didn't love being a priest.

The Camino has a way of letting things rise to the surface. Out here, with the noise stripped away, the truths you've tried to keep quiet start whispering louder. Today, they caught up with me. Tomorrow is a new stretch of road. A new sunrise. A new chance to listen, to heal, and to walk into grace—wherever it finds me.

A Downcast Soul, A Living God

As a deer longs for flowing streams, so my soul longs for you, O God. My soul thirsts for God, for the living God. When shall I come and behold the face of God? My tears have been my food day and night, while people say to me continually, "Where is your God?" These things I remember, as I pour out my soul: how I went with the throng, and led them in procession to the house of God, with glad shouts and songs of thanksgiving, a multitude keeping festival. Why are you cast down, O my soul, and why are you disquieted within me? Hope in God; for I shall again praise him, my help and my God.

—Psalm 42:1–6

On the Camino, there were days when the road brought more than just physical exhaustion. There were moments when the stillness—especially after long stretches of walking in solitude—brought a deeper kind of struggle. The journey, for all its beauty, sometimes led me into a confrontation with the quiet that held more than just silence; it held questions, especially questions about my vocation, my calling.

It was a struggle many of us face, I think. The moments when the joy of our work feels eclipsed by frustration or disappointment, when the sense of purpose we once had gets clouded by unresolved challenges. We may love the work we do yet feel disquieted by it. The very thing that once brought us joy becomes the source of a restless soul.

Reflecting on this day on the Camino, I couldn't help but think of Psalm 42, where David speaks of his soul being downcast, longing for God, yet feeling abandoned and distant from God. "Why are you cast down, O my soul, and why are you disquieted within me? Hope in God; for I shall again praise him, my help and my God" (Psalm 42:5–6). It's a powerful expression of the tension between love for God and the pain of feeling separated from God's peace. David's words resonated deeply as I walked through the landscape of my own questions, wondering if my vocation was still what I believed it to be.

Looking back, I realize that those moments of doubt were not the absence of faith, but an invitation to go deeper, to trust God with the parts of myself that were unsettled. It was a chance to lay down my doubts, knowing that even in those dark, questioning moments, God's grace was still enough.

Reflection Questions:

1. When have you experienced a struggle with your calling or purpose? How did you respond to it?

2. How do you handle moments of uncertainty or doubt in your journey of faith?
3. What might God be inviting you to let go of or trust him with today?

Lord, thank you for the space you provide in the quiet, where you invite us to wrestle with our deepest questions. Help me to trust you in moments of doubt and to find peace in knowing you are with me, even when I can't see the way forward. May I embrace the struggle and walk forward in your grace.

Amen.

DAY 12

Santo Domingo and the Ongoing Questions

I got up late this morning—6:45 a.m., which out here almost feels like sleeping in. After a quick breakfast, I set out for Santo Domingo de la Calzada. The walk was peaceful and the day mercifully short. I arrived early, with enough time to shower, wash some clothes, and—luxury of luxuries—take a real siesta.

The physical rest was welcome, but the internal restlessness continued. I'm still carrying this unresolved tension around my vocation. Being a priest has been fulfilling, I know that with certainty—but what I'm doing now, the shape it's taken in recent months, has been difficult to love. Conflict weighs heavily.

I'm not walking to prove anything. I walk because I need to remember who I am beneath the pain. I keep asking, "What's next?" Out here, surrounded by vineyards and pilgrim songs and silence, that question echoes louder.

But grace came quietly today, in the form of a companion on the trail. Scott is a junior in college, majoring in biochemistry and possibly premed. We fell into step and then into a deep conversation about biological evolution and faith. It was one of those rare, unforced moments where intellect and belief intertwine naturally. We didn't debate—we shared. It felt rich, honest, and important. Scott asked what I did for a living, and I dodged the question with what has become my pat answer, "I went through a bad situation at work, so if you don't mind, I'd rather talk about anything other than my work." Thus far, it has protected my anonymity.

Later, after resting, I made my way to the plaza to write and plan for the next leg of my journey. As I scribbled in my journal, Mona wandered by and we decided to grab beers at a tavern nearby. Rain began to fall, soft and steady, and soon Mary and Maura joined us. Before they arrived, Mona and I ended up in a long, thoughtful conversation about religion—her distance from it, and my faith within it. I'm continually amazed at the skepticism, sometimes outright negativity, toward religion I've encountered on the Camino. It doesn't discourage me, but it does make me more convinced of the need for what the writer of Hebrews wrote: being ready to give an answer for the hope that is within us. Not an argument. An answer—something real, lived, and alive.

In the plaza this evening, we were entertained by a group of college-aged minstrels from Pennsylvania, walking the Camino with nothing but their voices, their feet, and whatever food and lodging they could beg for along the way as they performed. There's something both wild and holy about that. It reminds me that this journey isn't just physical or even spiritual—it's something ancient, something shared, something beautiful.

I don't know what tomorrow holds. Today was full in its own way—full of questions, of good conversation, of rain, and of little revelations. The road continues, and I'll keep walking.

A Reason for Hope

"For the eyes of the Lord are on the righteous, and his ears are open to their prayer. But the face of the Lord is against those who do evil." Now who will harm you if you are eager to do what is good? But even if you do suffer for doing what is right, you are blessed. Do not fear what they fear, and do not be intimidated, but in your hearts sanctify Christ as Lord. Always be ready to make your defense to anyone who demands from you an accounting for the hope that is in you; yet do it with gentleness and reverence.

—1 Peter 3:12–16

Looking back, what stays with me from that day in Santo Domingo isn't the ease of the walk or the blessing of rest, but the deeper restlessness I carried within. Even with our questions, grace has a way of finding us, not always in resolution, but in encounter. Conversations that day reminded me that people rarely ask for theological precision. They ask for hope, especially when the Christian story feels distant or damaged. They don't need an argument. They need to know whether belief still holds any relevance in a world as fractured as this one.

Real hope is not passive or naive. It is born of grief and longing. It names what is broken and still dares to believe in restoration. It gives us the courage to keep walking—even when we're not sure what's ahead.

In that season of personal pain on the Camino, in my conversations with Scott and Mona, I wasn't trying to explain my faith. In truth, I was guarding what remained of it. Even in that guardedness, I found myself offering something—just by being present, by listening, by sharing life with fellow pilgrims. That, too, was a witness. Not the kind that shouts, but the kind that stays.

When the Church fails, when institutions wound, when belief is tested, we are still called to live in such a way that others might catch a glimpse of hope, not as a concept, but as a lived conviction. When asked, we are called to speak of it—not with defensiveness, but with gentleness and respect. I couldn't have named it then, but I see it clearly now: Even on days when faith felt thin, hope still showed up. When hope made itself known, it was enough.

Reflection Questions:

1. When have you carried faith quietly, even while wrestling with doubt?
2. What does it mean to give a reason for hope without needing to defend it?
3. Who might need your presence more than your certainty?

God of the questions and the road,
you meet us in our weariness
and you walk with us in our wondering.
When we cannot offer answers, help us offer honesty.
When hope is hard to name, help us to live it.
Give us courage to face what is,
and grace to trust in what can be.
And when the time comes to speak,
may our words be gentle, true, and filled with light.

Amen.

DAY 13

Wrestling and Revelation on the Camino

Last night, I attended Mass at the cathedral with Maura, my Roman Catholic friend from Virginia. Only she and her daughter Mary know I'm a priest. When they mentioned that they were from Virginia, before I could catch myself, I mentioned that I went to seminary in Alexandria. They promised to keep my secret, and thus far they have been true to their word. Maura is deeply spiritual, intelligent, and grounded in faith. I considered asking her to hear my confession, even though she is not a priest. Our paths have separated again—she stayed in Belorado, and I pressed on another six kilometers before the rain caught up to me. Before I left Belorado, I took a photo of Martin Sheen's hand and foot imprint. Somehow, that felt symbolic—a reminder of all who have walked this way before me.

God's been working on me hard these last few days—and I say that in the most loving, honest way I can. It hasn't been easy, but there's a grace in the struggle. After a good night's sleep, I woke up sore but refreshed. Physically, my body is beginning to call for rest. I walked thirty kilometers today, all the way to Villambistia. All the while, there have been questions in my mind about my life in the Church, and about the effectiveness of the Church in proclaiming the gospel to an ever more secular culture. I've met so many people on this path with no spiritual compass, no grounding in faith. It breaks my heart. Not just for them, but for us—the Church. We've not always been there to respond when the world has been crying out.

But these conversations, these moments of raw honesty with fellow pilgrims—especially the younger ones like David and Elizabeth, stir something in me. I am given a vision of the kind of priest I want to be. Given a sense of what kind of Church we're called to become. Not a Church applying new marketing techniques to stay relevant, but one rooted in love, in presence, in authenticity.

Walking beside the highway the other day, I was struck by the contrast: cars rushing by, unconscious and fast; us pilgrims moving slowly, intentionally, and aware. That's an apt metaphor for the Church right now—while life is overwhelming for many, we need to be the ones who walk beside others, who see their pain, who speak meaningfully into their lives.

God gave me a gift today. As I wrestled, God reminded me that temptation, that testing, is an opportunity—a chance to affirm who we truly are. Jesus's temptation in the wilderness wasn't punishment; it was confirmation of his sonship. I'm seeing that now. My demons are not me. The thorn in my flesh—I know it well—is always with me. However, the deeper it digs, the more I'm reminded of who I am in Christ. I am a beloved son.

The Gift of the Struggle

Then Jesus was led up by the Spirit into the wilderness to be tempted by the devil. He fasted forty days and forty nights, and afterwards he was famished. The tempter came and said to him, "If you are the Son of God, command these stones to become loaves of bread." But he answered, "It is written, 'One does not live by bread alone, but by every word that comes from the mouth of God.'" Then the devil took him to the holy city and placed him on the pinnacle of the temple, saying to him, "If you are the Son of God, throw yourself down; for it is written, 'He will command his angels concerning you,' and 'On their hands they will bear you up, so that you will not dash your foot against a stone.'" Jesus said to him, "Again it is written, 'Do not put the Lord your God to the test.'"

—Matthew 4:1–7

One of the greatest lies our temptations tell us is that we are what we wrestle with. That our struggle somehow disqualifies us from grace or distances us from God. In the wilderness—whether in a spiritual desert or on a Camino trail—we are often reminded that temptation doesn't define us. It reveals us. When I look back on that day of walking, wrestling, and longing, I see now how God wasn't absent in my questions—God was pressing in through them. Though disquieted in the very depths of my soul, with every step, I sensed a strange and refining grace.

In the quiet companionship of fellow pilgrims—especially the young seekers like David and Elizabeth—something stirred: a longing not just to remain a priest, but to become a more authentic one. Not polished. Not defensive. A priest grounded in presence and love, able to speak not at others but with them. To be real. That day on the Camino, I began to see my struggles in a new light—not as disqualifications, but as confirmations. Jesus' temptation didn't happen in spite of his identity as the Son of God, but because of it. The testing didn't make him more divine—it proved that he already was. The same Spirit who led Jesus into the wilderness did not abandon him there.

I realized that the voice that says, "If you are . . ." is not God's voice. God's voice says, "You are my beloved." Full stop. There's no necessity to prove it. To live authentically is not to live unchallenged. It is to live honestly, humbly, and vulnerably in the face of temptation and still return again and again to the deeper truth: I am not what tempts me. I am not what wounds me. I am not the sum of my fears or failures. I am God's, and that is enough.

The slow, deliberate steps of the Camino mirror this deeper way. In a world that rushes past pain and complexity, the call of Christ is to move differently—to walk with awareness, to notice, to love, and to live not for performance but for presence. We are not here to race; we are here to walk with others, and to remember who we truly are. I still carry my "thorn in the flesh." I still hear the questions, but more than anything, I remember that day as a day I remembered who I was.

Reflection Questions:

1. What voices in your life have tried to define you by your struggles?
2. How has wrestling with temptation clarified—not clouded—your sense of identity?
3. What does it mean for you to live authentically in your current context?

Jesus, you were not ashamed of the wilderness.
You did not shrink from struggle,
and you never forgot who you were.
When I am tempted to believe I am less than your beloved,
remind me again of what is true.
Teach me to walk in step with you—slow, present, unafraid.
Shape me not through certainty, but through faithfulness.

Amen.

DAY 14

Bones, Bread, and the Sound of Many Nations

Last night's dinner offered another Camino moment of unexpected grace. I found myself at a table with four Spaniards. Only one of them spoke a little English, but that didn't stop them from making sure I understood something they clearly felt mattered: "It was the Hispanic vote that elected Obama," they declared. The message was simple, direct, delivered with smiles and nods. I don't know why they wanted to make sure I knew that morsel of insight, but I received it with gratitude. There's a human need to be seen—and politics, like faith, often carries layers far deeper than the surface conversation. The evening meal was otherwise simple but meaningful—as most Camino meals tend to be. My companions and I did what we could with gestures and shared laughter, language barriers giving way to the common ground of bread, wine, and the day's exhaustion.

This morning, I didn't eat until I'd walked for six kilometers—two hours before anything touched my stomach. I know, I said earlier that I would never let that happen again but I'm a slow learner. My body let me know how displeased it was with me. Still, it was a beautiful walk. For the most part, the path drifted away from the highway and into the woods. There's something sacred about that—the silence of trees, the rhythm of feet on the path. The final six kilometers led me to Atapuerca. I had planned to push further, but the lodging ahead looked uncertain, so I stayed. Showered. Washed my clothes. Now, with a bag of chips, I sit in the quiet of the early evening, just trying to be still.

Most of my Camino companions are now behind me. Only Adam and Joanne are possibly still ahead of me. That sense of community I felt in the early days has shifted. Now, I enter true isolation—just me and my thoughts. I'm noticing how many of my thoughts are recycled, how often I return to the same questions, the same worries, the same memories. Maybe that's part of the work here—the way the Camino presses you into your own mind long enough to actually hear yourself.

When I arrived in Atapuerca, I almost didn't stop. I passed the albergue thinking I'd keep going. Then I took a moment at a fountain to refill my water. An old man passed by, a loaf of bread under his arm, and without hesitation, sat next to me. He began speaking—probably telling me about his village. I couldn't understand a word, but it didn't matter. There was kindness in his voice, warmth in his eyes. He didn't need me to understand—only to receive the moment. People are the true gift of the Camino. Today I met a multi-generational family from Florida. Three generations walking the Camino. Judy, the grandmother—seventy-one years old and walking her third Camino.

Today I visited the tomb of Saint Juan de Ortega. The church there was quite stunning—intricate works of art, and curiously, carvings of dogs behind the altar. Odd, but beautiful. Sacred spaces along the Camino feel like little altars on the side of the road—places where time folds in on itself and reminds you that you're not the first to walk this way, and you won't be the last.

Tonight, like many other nights, the pilgrims gathered in the bar to watch the European Cup. It's become a kind of ritual. The Netherlands, South Africa, Spain, Australia, Finland, Germany, and two North Americans, a Canadian and me—all huddled around a TV, shouting in a multitude of languages, cheering, groaning, laughing. Honestly? I'm becoming a soccer fan. There's a magic in these shared moments, when strangers from across the world become teammates for a night. It's strange, this dance between solitude and community. On one hand, I miss the friends I started with. On the other, I find a strange peace in walking alone, in meeting new faces every day, in these brief but rich encounters.

Atapuerca, it turns out, is also a paleontology center. Nearby discoveries have turned it into a hub for the study of ancient bones—humanity's distant ancestors buried deep in the earth. It's strange to be sitting above the bones of people who walked before language, before maps, before roads. Here I am, thousands of years later, walking for reasons they couldn't have imagined, yet somehow walking the same earth.

Tomorrow, I hope to reach Burgos. I'm ready for a rest. Maybe some stillness. There's a lot of downtime on the Camino. Your feet can only take you so far, and then all that's left is waiting—for food, for sleep, for tomorrow, for whatever comes next. Sometimes, waiting becomes its own kind of joy. In my waiting, my mind often drifts back home and I think of Pamela. The more I remember what a gift she is in my life, the more I long to see her again. The road stretches out in front of me, but sometimes it feels like it's stretching back to her. I can't wait until she joins me in Sarria.

The God Who Sees

After this I looked, and there was a great multitude that no one could count, from every nation, from all tribes and peoples and languages, standing before the throne and before the Lamb, robed in white, with palm branches in their hands. They cried out in a loud voice, saying, "Salvation belongs to our God who is seated on the throne, and to the Lamb!" And all the angels stood around the throne and around the elders and the four living creatures, and they fell on their faces before the throne and worshiped God, singing, "Amen! Blessing and glory and wisdom and thanksgiving and honor and power and might be to our God forever and ever! Amen."

—Revelation 7:9–12

That evening in Atapuerca lingers as one of those quietly radiant Camino moments—unplanned, deeply human, and mysteriously sacred. Even across language barriers and continents, my dinner companions wanted to be known—and I think that desire lives in all of us.

As I reflect on their need to be seen, I think of the story of Hagar, who is with her son Ishmael in the wilderness, dismissed by Abraham due to the jealousy of Sarah. The first naming of God in the Bible happens. In that moment, she names God as "the God who sees me." Isn't that the desire of us all, to be seen by others, to be seen by God? So often, we think of communion as bread and wine passed around a sanctuary. That night, however, it was laughter over soup, hand gestures, broken sentences, and the fatigue of a shared journey.

Communion was the warmth in a stranger's eyes and the sense that even across cultures, we all carry stories that matter.

Atapuerca itself is built upon bones—some of the oldest human remains in Europe were unearthed there. I didn't realize it then, but the Camino was teaching me that our walk is always part of a larger story—across time, across cultures, across languages. The saints. The strangers. The scientists and pilgrims. The soccer fans gathered in bars. The old man with a loaf of bread who sat next to me without needing a reason. These are the great multitude. In their presence, I caught a glimpse of what John described in Revelation: a chorus of nations, each voice distinct, yet joined in a single holy song.

This leg of the journey marked a transition for me. I was entering a season of deeper solitude, and with it came the echo of familiar thoughts—some joyful, others troubling. I've learned since then that silence has its own voice. The Camino quiets you long enough to hear it. We often think of waiting as wasted time. On the Camino, I discovered that waiting could become its own act of worship. In the waiting, we remember. We anticipate. We hope, and in our hoping sometimes we are gifted with glimpses of heaven—a shared meal with strangers, laughter in many tongues, and love that draws us forward.

Reflection Questions:

1. When have you experienced a moment of unexpected connection across cultural or linguistic divides?

2. What does it mean to you to be part of a "great multitude" that transcends time and place?

3. Revelation 7, the scripture above, offers a vision of a great multitude—people from every nation and language worshipping together. How does your experience of community reflect (or fall short of) that vision?

God of many nations and ancient paths, thank you for the unexpected grace of connection. Thank you for the bread we break with strangers. Remind me that I am part of a vast story—larger than language, deeper than distance, and held together in you. In every longing, in every silence, and in every shared moment, help me listen for the sacred.

Amen.

Purgation

DAY 15

Cathedrals, Crosses, and Cold-Water Grace

Climbing out of Atapuerca today, we crested a hill where someone—or many someones—had built something elaborate from stone. At the top was a cross, simple and bold, and below it, a labyrinth, carefully laid out by pilgrims before me. I didn't walk it. Not because I wasn't moved by it, but because I'm currently walking my own pilgrimage. In the Middle Ages many Christians who could not make a pilgrimage to Jerusalem, Rome, Santiago, or other pilgrim sites would walk labyrinths to be a proxy for their desired pilgrimages, with the center of the labyrinth symbolic of Jerusalem.

Today's hike brought me through Burgos, the capital of Castilla—a city full of noise, movement, and towering beauty. The Gothic cathedral there is stunning—a marvel of craftsmanship and quiet reverence. Worth every bit of the €3.50 it took to step inside. I didn't linger too long in the city, though. The Camino has a rhythm, and I've found I'm more at home now in its quieter stretches. Leaving Burgos, the path followed a river that slices through the city. It was beautiful—water flowing steadily beneath footbridges, trees leaning in to offer shade.

Once again, my American sensibilities were shocked as I saw women sunbathing topless along the banks, as free as the breeze. One of those moments where you realize the Camino is a string of contrasts: sacred and sensual, silent and loud, deeply interior and yet fully alive to the world around you.

I walked twenty-nine kilometers today—a long day, but a good one. I ended up in Tardajos, a small village west of Burgos, and found a lovely little albergue. Simple, quiet, run by volunteers from Madrid. The couple hosting this week were not from Madrid, however, but from Bellingham, Washington. Often, people who have previously walked the Camino will come back to serve pilgrims as hospitaleros. Funny how the Camino pulls people across oceans and decades into this strange, sacred fellowship.

After I'd showered and laid out my clothes to dry, Rose invited me to soak my feet in a foot bath—cold water, salt, and vinegar. It's meant to prevent swelling, and though I haven't had any real issues with my feet, my joints tell a different story. My knees and hips ache most nights. The pain is a kind of prayer in itself—a reminder that this is a pilgrimage of the body as much as the spirit.

I'm learning that I prefer the smaller villages to the big city stops. There's something about them—they're quieter, more human scale. These small villages do, however, still create a certain discomfort for me as a pilgrim, a stranger traipsing through their tight-knit community. You wonder what the locals think of us, these dusty wanderers taking over their town for a night. Maybe it's part of the Camino too—walking through both welcome and resistance, finding grace in both.

Tonight, as I sit and stretch and sip, I think again of Pamela. Of Judy walking her third Camino. Of the man with the bread. Of labyrinths made by unseen hands. Of cathedrals rising from the ground and feet soaking in vinegar water. This is a hard road, but it's a good one.

Grace in the Foreign Place

All of these died in faith without having received the promises, but from a distance they saw and greeted them. They confessed that they were strangers and foreigners on the earth, for people who speak in this way make it clear that they are seeking a homeland. If they had been thinking of the land that they had left behind, they would have had opportunity to return. But as it is, they desire a better country, that is, a heavenly one. Therefore God is not ashamed to be called their God; indeed, he has prepared a city for them.

—Hebrews 11:13–16

Some of the most spiritually formative moments on the Camino didn't come through comfort or acceptance, but through the unease of being a stranger. That day, I had walked through the city of Burgos, past its magnificent cathedral, through bustling streets filled with people who barely noticed the weary pilgrims passing by. Even beauty, I discovered, could feel distant.

And yet, I never fully escaped the feeling of being out of place. In small villages and big cities alike, I often felt like an outsider, unsure of how I was perceived. We pilgrims moved through their world like shadows—visible, present, but never fully part of the scene. I had wondered then: Was the discomfort theirs . . . or mine? In time, I began to see that this very discomfort was shaping me. There was a stripping away that happened in those moments—of identity, of ego, of the need to be understood. I no longer had the comforts of home, the protection of titles, or even the ease of familiar language. I was just one more pilgrim on the Camino, aching joints, dusty clothes, and a heart that was slowly learning to open.

It struck me how often God had used this experience—the experience of being a foreigner—to shape his people. Again and again in Scripture, Israel was called to remember that they had once been strangers in Egypt. Their identity as a people was formed not just in liberation, but in the memory of displacement. That memory was meant to make them compassionate.

On that day of my journey I began to wonder what it meant to live with that kind of awareness—not just on pilgrimage, but in everyday life. To see myself as a guest in the world, and others as fellow pilgrims, regardless of where they called home. I thought of the unseen hands that laid out labyrinths and built footbaths, the quiet grace of locals who opened their villages—and sometimes their hearts. I see now that those foreign places, those foreign feelings, had been holy ground all along.

Reflection Questions:

1. How do you respond to situations where you feel overlooked, misunderstood, or out of place?
2. What role does discomfort play in your spiritual growth?
3. In what ways might God be inviting you to welcome the "stranger" in your life or community?

God of the stranger and sojourner, thank you for the grace that meets us in unfamiliar places. Strip away the need to be known and let me find comfort in being known by you alone. Teach me to walk humbly when I am the outsider and to welcome others with the same compassion you have shown me. May every ache, every misunderstanding, every quiet village remind me that I belong not to the world's applause but to your pilgrim path.

Amen.

DAY 16

Cool Mornings, Hot Winds, Unexpected Drama

I'm truly growing to love the Meseta. The mornings start off cool and crisp, perfect for walking, and the afternoons turn hot but are softened by a steady, refreshing wind. The landscape is relatively flat, which makes for great progress. I made excellent time and distance today, covering thirty-one kilometers before stopping in Castrojeriz for the night.

As always, it's the people who add color to the journey. Along the way, I met Carol from Germany and Leanna from Denmark. I also reconnected in Hornillos del Camino with a mother and son from Austin, Texas—Barbara and Jordan—who introduced me to a wonderful Australian pilgrim named Dooley. Dooley is traveling with three women: Sarah and Anna, both from Spain, and Greta, who had a sharp sense of humor.

As I walked, I found myself playing with the sun and my shadow as a metaphor for my life with Christ. When the sun (Jesus) is behind me, I can see the shadow—it's big and noticeable. However, when the sun is overhead, the shadow shrinks, barely visible. When the sun is in front of me, when my eyes are on Jesus, the shadow still exists, but it's behind me—out of sight, yet still part of me. A simple metaphor, but one that resonated deeply with me on the trail today.

The night at our albergue took a strange turn. I was relaxing on my bunk when Emma—an English woman I'd met that morning at the previous night's albergue—walked in with her boyfriend. Her assigned bunk was located above mine. Her boyfriend, half-drunk and clearly not thrilled about not being on the bunk below Emma, immediately became suspicious. He demanded to know why I was sleeping below Emma instead of him and then launched into accusations, suggesting I had been inappropriate with her—which, in a crowded albergue, was laughable. Emma tried to calm him down, reminding him that we had met that morning at our previous albergue. The problem was we hadn't. More than likely he was still nursing the previous night's hangover when Emma and I met. He fired back at her in French, presumably so I wouldn't understand.

He left the room with her and eventually returned by himself muttering "She's right, she's right," over and over, and then left the room again. I can only assume she assured him that she wanted nothing to do with an overweight, old American guy. Emma returned a short while later, apologized, explained that they had got in early and hit the bar. She then reassured me that they were going to get something to eat and he would be better when they returned.

I wasn't about to stick around and find out. Trusting my gut, after they left, I packed up quietly and slipped out, flip-flops on, boots in hand. I wandered the town looking for a bed—tried to find my friends from Austin, Texas, or the English group I'd chatted with earlier—with no luck. Every albergue was full. So once again, like Forrest Gump, I just started walking.

I left Castrojeriz, climbed a steep hill, got chased by three dogs (because why not, at this point), and ended up spending the night under the stars in the ruins of an old monastery that overlooks the town. It was cold and windy, and I won't pretend I got much sleep—but the sky was brilliant. On the ridge in front of me there were the blinking red warning lights of a line of windmills. Endlessly watching those lights against the backdrop of a starlit sky is something I will long remember. Of course, the fact that it was incredibly cold ensured I remained awake for the light show.

Betrayal, Shadows, and the God Who Is with Us

And Joseph's master took him and put him into the prison, the place where the king's prisoners were confined; he remained there in prison. But the LORD was with Joseph and showed him steadfast love; he gave him favor in the sight of the chief jailer. The chief jailer committed to Joseph's care all the prisoners who were in the prison, and whatever was done there, he was the one who did it. The chief jailer paid no heed to anything that was in Joseph's care, because the LORD was with him; and whatever he did, the Lord made it prosper.

—Genesis 39:20–23

Long before I reached that hilltop outside Castrojeriz, I was already carrying a heavy burden—not just the weight of false accusations made against me, but also the more honest realization that I hadn't handled everything well myself. A professional rupture had left my reputation bruised and my spirit frayed. I had made mistakes and in hindsight, I learned the wisdom of the saying, "Praise in public, criticize in private." I came to the Camino hoping that the long miles and wide skies might offer clarity, maybe even healing. I quickly learned that a pilgrimage doesn't free you from what you carry inside; it just gives you space to face it.

So when I found myself again accused—this time by a stranger with too much suspicion and too little sobriety—it cut deeper than the moment itself. It wasn't simply the discomfort of being misunderstood. It was the way it mirrored the earlier wound. His accusations stung, because they reopened something I thought I had started to move past. Years later, I still hesitate to name it, because naming it means revisiting the sting of it. Jesus wasn't betrayed by a stranger or an enemy, but by one of his own. A disciple. A companion. One who shared bread with him. That's what makes betrayal so devastating: its intimacy. That's also what makes it so hard to heal from.

As I reflected under the stars that night—cold, tired, and alone—I remembered the image that had come to me earlier that day. Walking with the sun behind me, my shadow was always in front—looming, exaggerated, unavoidable. When the sun was directly overhead, the shadow shrank. When the sun was in front of me, the shadow followed behind—still there, but no longer my focus.

It struck me then: Shame always wants to lead. It pushes itself into the foreground, demanding our attention, even when it has no rightful claim. As Brené Brown writes, "Shame corrodes the very part of us that believes we are capable of change."[4] That's what it does—it hijacks the narrative, convincing us we're defined by our worst mo-

---

4. Brené Brown, *I Thought It Was Just Me (But It Isn't): Making the Journey from "What Will People Think?" to "I Am Enough"* (Gotham Books, 2007), 197.

ments. When we choose to walk with Christ in front of us—when we set our gaze on him—the shadows don't disappear, but they lose their power. They fall behind.

I thought of Joseph, unjustly accused in Egypt, thrown into prison for a crime he didn't commit. His integrity didn't prevent the suffering, but it shaped his endurance. The Bible doesn't tell us that God spared him from injustice—it tells us that "the Lord was with" Joseph. That's what I began to understand that night. I wasn't alone, and my story wasn't defined by anyone other than God. The Camino didn't erase the wounds I carried, but it did remind me that healing doesn't require everyone to see the truth—as long as God does, and God did.

Reflection Questions:

1. Have you ever contributed to a rupture in a relationship through your own actions or words? What might you do differently in hindsight?
2. What "shadows" from your past do you still carry? How do they show up in your life?
3. What does it look like for you to let Jesus walk in front of you today?

God of mercy and truth, you see beyond appearances and know my heart. When shame tries to lead, help me remember that you walk ahead of me, casting light on the path and leaving shadows behind. Heal what accusation has broken in me and teach me to rest in the truth that I am yours.

Amen.

DAY 17

A Place of Transition and the Road Beyond

In spite of a restless, sleepless night spent under the stars in the cold, I managed to walk thirty-five kilometers today to Villarmentero de Campos. My feet were tired, but my spirit felt strangely alive. The landscape remains wide and open, the Meseta stretching ahead like a quiet invitation to go deeper, not just into Spain, but into myself.

Along the way, I had good company. Edwina, who goes by Ed, a British woman with a thoughtful presence, walked with me for a stretch, and we shared a deep conversation about the spirituality of the Camino—how it shapes you, speaks to you, and somehow strips away the excess. Later, I was joined by Emily from Paris, and a kind woman from China, now living in the Netherlands, whose name sadly escapes me. The Chinese woman moved on ahead, but Emily and I walked together.

We stopped at an albergue in Villarmentero de Campos—eclectic and full of character. Think of Bob Marley posters and colorful mismatched chairs. It had the feeling of a place that didn't take itself too seriously, and maybe that's what we needed. We had dinner together, sharing laughs and wine and stories with other pilgrims. Among them was another

French woman, also from Paris, fluent in French, English, and Spanish. She generously played translator, as some of the Spanish women were curious—Why is an American walking the Camino? It's getting easier to answer. I'm in a place of transition. Trying to sort out the way forward—career, life, faith. I don't know exactly what I'm moving toward, but I know I'm leaving something behind. Which is perhaps the point.

Over dinner, one pilgrim shared a metaphor that stuck with me. He said the Camino can be seen in stages: From Saint-Jean-Pied-de-Port to Burgos is a time of letting go. Burgos to León, the area known as the Meseta, is a time of purgation—of walking through a kind of interior desert. Then, the mountain climb to Cruz de Ferro is the dying to self, and beyond that, resurrection. I pray that for myself. As I walk, it becomes more than just distance or destination. It's about the people, the conversations—deep and surprising—and the stillness in between. It's overwhelming at times, in the best way.

Today, I also came across an unforgettable albergue in Puente Fitero. The albergue was built inside what was once a hospital for *peregrinos*. It was a stone structure with a timber Gothic ceiling—sacred and simple. An altar stood at one end, a wooden balcony at the other. Three icons rested at the altar, illuminated by candlelight. There was no electricity—just a gas stove for cooking and a gentle hush in the air. The Italian confraternity that runs it welcomed each of us with warm, quiet hospitality. It felt like a sanctuary. Not just a place to sleep, but a place to be. This journey continues to surprise me—not just with its physical demands, but with its ability to carve out something new inside. I can't quite name it yet, but I feel it happening.

Trusting the Work Beneath the Surface

Indeed, everything is for your sake, so that grace, when it has extended to more and more people, may increase thanksgiving, to the glory of God. So we do not lose heart. Even though our outer nature is wasting away, our inner nature is being renewed day by day. For our slight, momentary affliction is producing for us an eternal weight of glory beyond all measure, because we look not at what can be seen but at what cannot be seen, for what can be seen is temporary, but what cannot be seen is eternal.

—2 Corinthians 4:15 18, NRSVUE

Until that stretch of the Camino, I had thought of healing as something linear, like walking from one village to the next: Leave something behind, cleanse the soul, die to self, and arrive reborn. I see now that the process of transformation is rarely that tidy. It's not a straight road; it's more like a spiral. You circle through familiar territory, but each time a little deeper, a little truer.

I remember that day as a turning point, not because of some dramatic revelation, but because of a quiet, growing awareness. I was in a place of transition—not just geographically, but spiritually. Something in me was loosening its grip. There was no sudden clarity about my future, no divine voice telling me which road to take. There was a gentle invitation to trust the work happening beneath the surface.

In the years since, I've come to think of that season on the Meseta as a long exhale. Life had been full of striving and hurt, of unspoken grief and unanswered questions. I had come to the Camino carrying wounds. The Camino didn't magically erase them, but it did offer needed space. Space to be still. Space to be honest. Space to begin the long, slow work of releasing what no longer served the person I was becoming.

That's the spiritual path, isn't it? Not a single act of surrender, but a lifetime of shedding layers. I've had to learn this over and over: The process of purgation isn't punishment, it's grace. It's God gently drawing us out of the versions of ourselves we've outgrown, even the ones that once protected us.

One image from that day has stayed with me: a simple albergue, candlelit and sparse, nestled in what used to be a pilgrim hospital. It wasn't grand or comfortable, but it was holy. A space that asked nothing of me except presence. I see it now as a picture of God's hospitality—an invitation to come as I was, with no need to perform or explain. Paul writes, "Though outwardly we are wasting away, yet inwardly we are being renewed day by day" (2 Corinthians 4:16, NIV). That renewal often happens quietly, hidden beneath the daily dust and ache, but it is happening. It was happening, even then. Sometimes the greatest grace isn't in reaching the next milestone. It's in realizing that healing doesn't require resolution. It requires trust.

Reflection Questions:

1. Are you resisting a stage of your spiritual journey—letting go, purgation, dying to self?

2. What layer of self-protection might God be gently asking you to shed?

3. Where in your life do you sense God's quiet invitation simply to be?

God of the long road and hidden renewal, thank you for meeting me in the spaces in between—when I'm no longer who I was, and not yet who I will become. Teach me to trust the process of becoming, even when it feels slow or uncertain. Give me courage to let go, to walk through the desert places, and to welcome each small rebirth as a sign of your grace at work within me.

Amen.

DAY 18

Purgation on the Meseta

Today's walk covered about twenty-seven kilometers, though it felt longer—especially the stretch that seemed to roll on forever through a landscape that could've been borrowed straight from Kansas. The tedium set in quickly, and with it, the perfect backdrop for reflection. According to the Italian pilgrim I met yesterday, this part of the Camino—the Meseta—is a time of purgation. As the scenery blurred into sameness and the rhythm of my steps settled into the silence, I began to ask: What am I meant to purge?

That's when the anger surfaced. Suddenly, and without warning, I was gripped by a wave of fury—anger about the professional impasse I had come to. The intensity of the anger caught me off guard, how raw it was. Maybe that's the grace of this part of the walk: to bring these hidden resentments into the light so I can lay them down at Cruz de Ferro. What a gift that would be—to truly let it go, to leave it behind and walk lighter.

If my professional path is stunted, then I find myself asking: How does God redeem this part of my story? How does God bring beauty from what has felt like failure, shame, and loss? Yet, if not for my spiritual turmoil, I wouldn't be here. So perhaps part of the redemption is the Camino itself—the space, the silence, the reflection. The chance to be unhurried and unhidden.

Along today's path, I had a meaningful conversation with Mylsis, a young Parisian who recently completed university and is now doing consulting work in organizational change. We spent nearly an hour talking about the business world, the nature of change, and, eventually, the Camino itself. I kept quiet about my own role as a church leader—it felt more important to listen, to engage without assumption. As we talked, the conversation turned spiritual. She mentioned how the infrastructure of the Camino—albergues, signposts, cafés—frees the pilgrim from having to worry about survival, giving them space to reflect. I shared that, for those of us from liturgical traditions, our worship functions in the same way. The repetition, the rhythm—it's the infrastructure that makes space for God to speak. It's not the structure that moves us, but the room it creates for something sacred to happen.

These kinds of moments—openhearted conversations with curious, reflective young people—remind me of something I've long desired: to serve as a spiritual mentor at this stage of my life. I think of young adults in my church, and I wonder—what if I could be someone who young people seek out not because of my title, but because of my presence? Because I listen, because I've walked a few roads ahead?

I'm spending the night in Calzadilla de la Cueza. The albergue here even has a swimming pool—an unexpected blessing on Father's Day. We ended the evening with a simple but joyful dinner. I sat with Mylsis, Hilary from Ireland, and Kasch from the Netherlands, who has walked all the way here from his home. These shared meals are sacred too—filled with laughter, stories, and languages overlapping across the table like music.

Kasch remembered me from the albergue in Castrojeriz two days ago where I had escaped Emma's drunk boyfriend. He asked what had happened to me, as one moment I was there, the next I was gone. As I recounted the events of that afternoon he started to laugh uncontrollably. Kasch reported that Emma must have really torn into her boyfriend because the whole night they could hear him saying to Emma over and over again, "I love you, Emma. I love you, Emma. I love you, Emma."

Letting Go of the Fire

How long, O LORD? Will you forget me forever? How long will you hide your face from me? How long must I bear pain in my soul, and have sorrow in my heart all day long? How long shall my enemy be exalted over me? Consider and answer me, O LORD my God! Give light to my eyes, or I will sleep the sleep of death, and my enemy will say, "I have prevailed"; my foes will rejoice because I am shaken. But I trusted in your steadfast love; my heart shall rejoice in your salvation. I will sing to the LORD, because he has dealt bountifully with me.

—Psalm 13:1–6

Years later, I can still remember the sharp clarity of that long, barren stretch of the Meseta. It wasn't the landscape that etched itself into my soul, but what it revealed. The silence, the sameness, the seemingly endless horizon—together they conspired to draw out something I had buried: anger. Not irritation. Not frustration, but real, guttural, soul-thick rage.

The betrayal I'd experienced back home rose up within me like a fire I could neither control nor ignore. In that moment, I was faced with the truth: I hadn't really let it go. I had managed it. Suppressed it. Even spiritualized it, but I hadn't surrendered it. I wasn't just angry, I was hurt.

And yet, scripture is no stranger to this kind of honesty. The Psalms are filled with the cries of a heart undone—"How long, O Lord?" (Psalm 13:1); "Break the teeth in their mouths, O God" (Psalm 58:6, NIV). David and the other psalmists never shied away from naming their fury, confusion, or grief. They didn't edit their prayers for theological correctness. They brought their rawness before God, trusting that God could handle it. That, perhaps, was the first step toward healing. I didn't understand that then, but I do now. Anger, left unresolved, doesn't just distort our view of others—it erodes our capacity to see God clearly. It poisons the well from which our spiritual life draws.

What surprised me most wasn't the anger itself. It was God's refusal to shame me for it. Instead, I sensed an invitation—bring it here, into the light. Let it surface in the silence. Let it pass through you like a storm. Let it go at the cross when the time comes. I didn't need to pretend I was farther along than I was. The Meseta allowed me to strip away any masks I was wearing.

I had once thought being the pastor of a large, corporate-size church or serving as a bishop would be the crowning work of my ministry. What if, however, the real call was something quieter, slower, less visible? What if the plans I held were simply scaffolding for something deeper God was building? The Camino taught me this: When our ambitions fall, space opens for deeper questions. Who am I without the role? Whose approval have I been chasing? What truly matters in the end?

Looking back, I see now that God wasn't withholding something from me. He was reshaping me. Not into a title or a position, but into a person—a mentor, a guide, a man at peace with being known for presence, not power. What I thought was failure was actually freedom. What I thought was fire meant to destroy was the fire that purifies.

Reflection Questions:

1. What unspoken anger or resentment are you carrying beneath the surface?
2. Where might God be inviting you to let go of titles or roles you once clung to?
3. How can you learn from the psalmist to express your emotions honestly before God?

God of holy fire and quiet redemption, you see the anger I carry and the plans I've clung to. Help me surrender both. Teach me to trust the road you've laid before me, even when it diverges from the one I hoped for. Strip away what no longer serves your purpose in me. Let my life reflect your grace, not through title or status, but through presence, humility, and love.

Amen.

DAY 19

Halfway, Hospitality, and Unholy Snoring

Hello from Sahagún. Today was . . . calm. After the last few days of dodging drunk boyfriends, escaping angry dogs, and wrestling with unexpected night hikes, "calm" feels like a small miracle. No drama. Just the usual Camino challenge: trying to get a good night's rest. Last night's challenge came courtesy of a fellow pilgrim who was already in bed when the rest of us returned from dinner—on his back, still fully clothed, and snoring to high heaven. He snored so violently, I'm fairly sure roof tiles were shaking, and he did not let up. I fell asleep to his thunder and woke up to the same relentless rhythm.

At one point, in a moment of half-asleep desperation, I genuinely considered crawling into his bunk to spoon him—hoping to roll him onto his side and end the thunderous snoring. There isn't enough beer in Spain. So, after a sleepless night and with a body running on fumes, I granted myself a little Camino grace and took it easy today—only twenty-two and a half kilometers, about fourteen miles. I've made such good time that if I don't slow down, I'll arrive in Sarria with days to spare and nothing but time to wait on Pamela.

The slower pace was actually kind of lovely. The road was quiet. I didn't pass many pilgrims—just a few scattered surprises. I ran into Kathleen from Ireland, who'd hopped ahead by taxi due to foot problems. It was good to catch up with her. I also spotted Emily and Kasch further down the trail. Familiar faces in unfamiliar places—one of the Camino's quiet gifts.

The walk gave me time to think. I dreamed a bit today—about church, about renewal. I found myself sketching out ideas for a fifth-Sunday worship service: something with more lay participation, a reimagined use of the worship space, a liturgy that invites the community into creativity and ownership. I even thought about organizing a Camino pilgrimage for the youth of East Texas. Imagine what it would be like for them to experience this rhythm of simplicity, reflection, and connection with God.

Once again, the quieter my surroundings as I walked, the louder the internal noise. My mind circled back again to the anger, the grief, the ache that's been my companion these past days. Still working through what all that means. Still in the purgation of the Meseta, I suppose.

Tonight, I'm staying at Ermita Virgen del Puente, just outside Sahagún. *Ermita* means chapel. It's a relatively new albergue set within the stone bones of an old church, part of a once-ambitious government initiative to restore chapels and turn them into pilgrim rest stops. Sadly, much of that work has stalled due to economic strain. The vision stays with me. It reminded me of the Church's older understanding of hospice—not as a place for the dying, but a shelter for the traveler. A sacred rest stop. A place where hospitality and holiness intertwine.

I passed the midway point on my pilgrimage today. Halfway to Santiago. Halfway through whatever God is doing in me. The second half awaits—hopefully with fewer snores, more insights, and continued whispers of God's presence along the way.

Rebuilding the Hospice Church

Come to me, all you that are weary and are carrying heavy burdens, and I will give you rest. Take my yoke upon you, and learn from me; for I am gentle and humble in heart, and you will find rest for your souls. For my yoke is easy, and my burden is light.

—Matthew 11:28–30

There is a kind of tiredness that sleep can't fix—the weariness of the soul. Many of us carry it: the weight of striving, disappointment, betrayal, or simply the fatigue of trying to hold everything together. The world rarely offers much relief for that kind of exhaustion. Sometimes, neither does the Church. What if the Church was meant to be something else entirely?

Historically, churches were not merely centers of worship or teaching—they were sanctuaries in the deepest sense. In the early Christian imagination, the Church was not just a place for the righteous to gather, but a refuge for the broken, the poor, the traveler. Saint Francis heard Christ's call to "rebuild my Church" while kneeling among the ruins of San Damiano. What he rebuilt was not just a structure, but a way of being—a community where the weary could breathe again, where holiness was clothed in humility and hospitality. Jesus spoke with the same intent when he said, "Come to me, all you that are weary and are carrying heavy burdens, and I will give you rest." He wasn't offering rest after people proved themselves worthy. He offered rest first—because rest is the beginning of restoration.

The albergue was humble, its stone walls weathered by time and the silence of long abandonment. Yet in that quiet space, I caught a glimpse of something sacred: a vision of the Church not as institution, but as shelter—a place for strangers to lay down their burdens and be welcomed with grace. Even in partial ruin, it spoke a deep truth: Hospitality is holy. Somewhere along the way, many churches have lost touch with this vision. We've become places of performance, pressure, and pretense, when we were meant to be havens of refuge, rhythm, and renewal. The tired, the skeptical, the burned out—they aren't looking for perfection. They're longing for room to exhale.

Perhaps it's time to return to a simpler calling: to make our churches more like spiritual hospices—sacred waystations on the road of life. Not only destinations of arrival, but places where weary pilgrims can find rest, safety, and strength for the journey ahead. Places where liturgy is not merely recited but embodied, where prayer opens space for honesty, and where wounded people are met not with shame but with blessing.

The Church will be rebuilt—not by better branding or busier calendars—but by people who understand this: Holiness is expressed through hospitality, and healing begins with welcome. Wherever you are today—wounded, wondering, or worn out—may you hear this invitation: Christ still welcomes the weary. Jesus still calls us to be the kind of Church that makes room for that rest to happen.

Reflection Questions:

1. When have you experienced the Church as a true place of rest and refuge?

2. Where is God calling you to create space for weary travelers—physically or spiritually?
3. What might it look like for your worship community to be a hospice?

Lord of the weary and the wandering,
You welcome us when we are tired, restless, and burdened.
Teach us to find our rest in you,
and to offer that same rest to others.
Rebuild your Church in us,
that it may become a shelter of grace,
a place where strangers are received as friends,
and the broken find space to breathe again.
Renew us with your gentleness,
so that we may carry lightness into the world.

Amen.

DAY 20

Sahagún to Reliegos

Today I walked about thirty-one kilometers from Sahagún to Reliegos. It was supposed to be a "resting" day—I'm ahead of schedule, so I gave myself the freedom to walk with no expectations. No pressure, no particular destination. Just the open road and the freedom to go as far or as little as I wanted. That sense of freedom made me reflect deeply—how often I live under the weight of expectations, both from others and from myself. The contrast today was refreshing and thought-provoking. I was reminded of Saint Paul's words: "For freedom Christ has set us free." (Galatians 5:1) Not the way my Camino friend Mona from the Netherlands understands it—a freedom without boundaries—but a deeper, richer freedom that comes when our lives, and all we long for, rest in God.

The Meseta continues to be a place of purgation for me—this wide, empty land seems to draw out everything hidden inside. Lately, it's been the purgation of anger. Yet, in this strange, sacred stretch of land, I can feel that anger rise within me without feeling guilty for embracing it. Maybe it's grace. Maybe it's the quiet acknowledgment of my own part in it all. Something in me is softening.

Along the way, I met a young couple from Elgin, Illinois. They were biking the Camino—full of energy and joy. It's strange how when I meet people from the Midwest it makes me feel as if I'm back in the Iowa hometown of my childhood. Our brief conversation was like a shot of espresso, giving me the lift I needed for the final six kilometers into Reliegos. Simple connections like that have become surprisingly meaningful out here.

I'm staying in a small albergue tonight, and I have just one roommate—a man walking the Camino on crutches. He's made the journey from Lourdes, France, to here in thirty-nine days. That alone puts my own complaints about aches and pains into perspective, but he's not well. He began feeling ill during our shared peregrino dinner—a beautifully international table with pilgrims from Spain, Portugal, France, and, of course, the United States. Tonight, I think he may be suffering from sunstroke, or perhaps something he ate. He's having a bad night. I'm concerned for him.

There's a new kind of isolation out here. Early in my pilgrimage, I intentionally embraced solitude. I loved it, relishing the quiet and space it offered. Today's solitude, on the other hand, was thrust upon me. It made me ask: Is solitude still a gift when it is forced on you? It made me think of the older members of my congregation who have lost spouses, of my mother-in-law who recently lost her husband of sixty-four years. I complain about being away from Pamela for four weeks, while they live with a separation that has no end on this side of eternity.

I thought about the Danny character from the 1981 movie *The Chosen*, starring Robby Benson in the lead role. Danny, the son of a Hasidic rabbi, was forced into silence and isolation from his father to learn compassion through pain. Maybe that's part of what this Camino is teaching me. To hurt, to heal, and to grow in mercy. As Philo of Alexandria wrote, "Be compassionate to everyone you meet—we are all fighting a great battle." Lord, help me to be more compassionate.

When Solitude Is No Longer a Choice

Turn to me and be gracious to me, for I am lonely and afflicted. Relieve the troubles of my heart and free me from my anguish. Look on my affliction and my distress and take away all my sins. See how numerous are my enemies and how fiercely they hate me! Guard my life and rescue me; do not let me be put to shame, for I take refuge in you. May integrity and uprightness protect me, because my hope, LORD, is in you.

—Psalm 25:16–21, NIV

Not all solitude is sacred—at least not at first. Some silence we choose: a retreat into stillness, the quiet of a slow morning, or the spaciousness of a long walk. I experienced that kind of holy solitude early in my Camino pilgrimage, when walking alone felt like freedom, like breathing more deeply than I had in years. There's another kind of solitude, the kind no one asks for. When that silence comes through grief, separation, or sorrow, it can feel more like exile than invitation.

On the Meseta, I felt it shift. What began as a day of rest—with no set distance or destination—slowly gave way to a deeper kind of emptiness. I had chosen the road, yes. I hadn't chosen this version of isolation. It wasn't peaceful anymore. It was hollow. The landscape around me—spacious, barren, stripped of noise—began to mirror what I felt inside. My anger surfaced again. In the absence of distraction, it demanded attention.

"Turn to me and be gracious to me, for I am lonely and afflicted. . . . Guard my life and rescue me," the psalmist prays in Psalm 25. I found myself echoing those words. They felt truer than anything I could have written myself. Like the psalmist, I was asking for God not only to see my pain, but to meet me in it. In that barren place, he began to do just that.

The solitude of the Meseta softened me, but not in the way I expected. It didn't bring comfort as much as it brought clarity. I thought of those who have lost loved ones, living with a permanent absence. Their solitude is not a retreat. It's a new terrain, uninvited and enduring. Psalm 25 reminds us, however, that God sees. God hears. God does not forsake the afflicted.

Even Jesus knew that kind of abandonment—when friends fell asleep in Gethsemane and heaven went silent at Calvary. If he passed through such silence and sanctified it, then perhaps our own loneliness is not without meaning. Forced solitude can be painful. It can also become sacred. If we let it, it may teach us compassion—not only for ourselves but for those around us who are quietly carrying far heavier loads.

Reflection Questions:

1. When have you experienced a solitude that wasn't chosen? How did it shape you?

2. Who in your life may be living in forced isolation today? How might you show them compassion?

3. Do you find it easier to sit with others in silence or to try to fix their pain?

Lord, you know the weight of unwanted silence and the ache of separation. In our loneliness, meet us with your presence. In our helplessness, grow in us compassion. Teach us to see not just our own solitude, but the unseen battles of those around us. Soften our hearts. Make us a people who sit with others in grace.

Amen.

DAY 21

León and La Virgen del Camino

This morning, I shared part of my walk with Emily, someone I hadn't seen for a few days. After a brief separation, we reunited just east of León. We had a small lunch at a park and then walked to the cathedral together. Kasch joined us when the cathedral opened for tours. Emily went her separate way to meet up with Bjorn, and I spent time exploring the beauty of the cathedral—from its stunning stained glass to the intricately carved woodwork in the quire.

The cathedral was simply incredible. While it wasn't as large as the cathedral in Burgos, it surpassed it in its magnificent stained glass. The light pouring through the windows gave the space an ethereal, sacred quality. It was truly something to behold. The beauty of the cathedral stood in stark contrast to the simplicity of my days walking the Camino, but it was a reminder of the sacredness in both.

Afterward, I left the city and met up with Kasch, who had found fellow pilgrims Fred and Hilary. We all stopped for a beer and had an interesting conversation about the Camino. Fred told me that every time he faces a big life decision, he walks a section of the Camino. It's something his family understands—it's a part of who he is. It felt like a providential meeting, and his story gave me much to reflect on.

As I walked, I once again reflected on my vocation. I questioned whether I want to remain at my church or if I should be open to new opportunities. I wrestled with how proactive I should be in my discernment—should I actively search for a new place, or wait and trust that God will bring it to me?

The Meseta has truly been a time of purgation for me, and I feel like I'm leaving behind anger and hurt. It has been days of deep introspection: What kind of Christian do I want to be? What kind of priest do I want to be? What kind of church do I want to be part of as I move forward in my life? The isolation of the Meseta is now behind me, but the reflections it brought continue. Many pilgrims skip this part of the Camino, taking a bus from Burgos to León, but I found the Meseta to be a rich and necessary time. I feel like I've left behind so much baggage from the past, and I look forward to what God has in store for me.

I'm so grateful for the prayers offered by friends back home concerning my lack of good sleep. Last night, I stayed at a small village albergue with only one other man in the room. He didn't snore, and I slept like a baby. A small mercy and much needed after a long day of walking. Today, I walked thirty-two kilometers and have arrived in La Virgen del Camino, on the west side of León. Now begins the ascent to Cruz de Ferro and a time of dying to self.

A Cathedral of Light

The LORD is my light and my salvation; whom shall I fear? The LORD is the stronghold of my life; of whom shall I be afraid? When evildoers assail me to devour my flesh—my adversaries and foes—they shall stumble and fall. Though an army encamp against me, my heart shall not fear; though war rise up against me, yet I will be confident. One thing I asked of the LORD, that will I seek after: to live in the house of the LORD all the days of my life, to behold the beauty of the LORD, and to inquire in his temple.

—Psalm 27:1–5

After days of stark horizons and interior wrestling, I stepped into the radiant heart of León's cathedral—and something in me shifted. The contrast was almost overwhelming. One moment, I was in the sparse quiet of an ancient landscape that had stripped me bare; the next, I was bathed in color and light that poured like grace through stained glass.

I remember standing still beneath the soaring Gothic arches, feeling small, humbled, and strangely seen. The architecture itself seemed to lift my eyes and spirit upward. Gothic cathedrals were designed for this—to evoke awe, to teach theology through stone and glass, and to awaken the soul to transcendence. Everything pointed to heaven, but it wasn't just grandeur for grandeur's sake. The beauty was built upon centuries of labor, sacrifice, and silence. Like the Camino.

In the cathedral, sunlight transformed as it passed through the windows. Mundane light became story—biblical scenes, saints, symbols—cast in jewel tones across the floor and pillars. That transformation mirrored what had been happening in me. For days, I had walked through the interior desert, confronting questions I couldn't answer.

The Meseta had been my place of purgation—dry, slow, and often lonely. It stripped away distractions and forced me to face the deeper layers of unresolved pain, vocational doubt, and the slow-burning embers of anger. I hadn't expected that part of the Camino. With the advantage offered by hindsight, I see its necessity. That season of spiritual austerity made the light of the cathedral all the more piercing. It was beauty as benediction.

I didn't leave León with clear answers. I left with quiet confidence that something had been shed, and something else was beginning to take root. In the rhythm of walking, in the companionships both fleeting and formative, in the silence I could no longer avoid, God had been at work. The Camino doesn't give easy resolutions, but it does offer clarity over time. Sitting in that cathedral, I was offered a moment of deep confirmation: The path of purgation is not in vain.

The cathedral marked not just a geographic turning point, but a spiritual one. From here, the terrain would begin to rise again. Ahead lay the mountains, the Cruz de Ferro, and what one pilgrim had described as the time of "dying to self." I used to think that phrase meant shedding ego or ambition, and perhaps it does. Now I wonder if it's even deeper than that. Perhaps it means letting go of the version of ourselves we've worked so hard to maintain. The curated self. The guarded self. The self that clings to certainty. Maybe dying to self is really about surrendering into mystery, trusting the unmarked path ahead, not because we understand it, but because God is already there.

Even now, years later, whenever I walk into a church with stained glass, I remember León. I remember how grace can find us at the edge of exhaustion, how light can preach a sermon, and how the spaces that shape us often come after the deserts that strip us.

Reflection Questions:

1. When have you experienced a "cathedral moment"—a time when beauty or sacred space pierced through your weariness and offered unexpected grace?
2. How does beauty—in art, architecture, or creation—speak to your soul? Where do you sense God most vividly through the senses?
3. What version of yourself have you carefully curated or protected? How might surrendering that self open you to deeper transformation?

God of glory,
you dwell in light no darkness can overcome.
You meet me not only in silence and struggle,
but in the beauty that catches me off guard and opens my heart.
Thank you for stained glass moments—
when ordinary light becomes something holy.
Let beauty be more than escape—
let it be encounter.
Lift my eyes toward the radiance of your presence,
and remind me that even in weariness,
you are preparing something new in me—
a city of light, already rising within.

Amen.

Dying to Self

DAY 22

Hospital de Órbigo

Today I traveled twenty-nine kilometers, with the longest uninterrupted stretch of my journey so far—a full ten kilometers without a break. The wind was in my face the entire time, and the hills returned, reminding me of the challenges behind me and those that lie ahead. It gave me a deeper appreciation for the line in the Irish blessing: "May the wind be always at your back." Today, the wind was definitely not at my back, but that only made the journey feel all the more significant.

This should be the last of the long, demanding days until Pamela arrives. Cruz de Ferro is now in sight, and I expect to reach it in about two days. Before ascending the path to Cruz de Ferro, I plan to stay the night at the monastery in a nearby town. It feels like a milestone, and as I draw closer to it, my thoughts have turned more toward what it means to die to self.

I've been reflecting on my own "thorn in the flesh"—that persistent struggle or weakness I carry with me. What would it be like to live without it? I remember a fellow priest, Mike Flynn, sharing that when he asked God to remove his own thorn, God's response was: "No—then you wouldn't need me." Saint Paul's thorn was never removed either, as far as we know from Scripture. Yet still, I wonder: Could I live a more victorious life if I didn't have to live with a "thorn in the flesh"? I know, however, that if I must live with it, I can find purpose in it. If nothing else, it's a constant reminder of my need for grace.

Tonight, I'm staying at a simple but lovely albergue in Hospital de Órbigo, one recommended by the peregrino website. It's quaint and peaceful, with some history, though I don't know much about it yet. The best part is that I arrived early enough to relax and unwind, giving me time to reflect. Sometimes the smallest pleasures, like a quiet moment in a beautiful place, are the most wonderful.

This afternoon, I focused on trying to learn balance in my life. I'm tempted to always push myself to churn out the kilometers, but today I reminded myself that rest is equally important. After a few moments of feeling a bit sorry for myself and the loneliness creeping in, I received a pleasant surprise. At dinner, I was joined by Charlie, a cyclist from Germany who's been doing the Camino all the way from his home country. We shared a meal, and it was nice to engage in good conversation.

Then, when I returned to the albergue, I passed a table of young Americans from Atlanta, Georgia. They invited me to join them for a chat—and for a radler, a new beverage for them. It's a refreshing mix of half beer, half lemon soda. *Radler* is the German word for cyclist, and this refreshing drink is often consumed by cyclists on their adventures. Conversation with fellow Americans in a language I understood was the perfect way to wrap up the evening. As I sit here reflecting on the day, I feel a sense of gratitude for these small, unexpected moments of connection. Tomorrow is a new day, with new challenges, but tonight, I'm content.

When Weakness Becomes the Way

To keep me from being too elated, a thorn was given to me in the flesh, a messenger of Satan to torment me, to keep me from being too elated. Three times I appealed to the Lord about this, that it would leave me, but he said to me, "My grace is sufficient for you, for power is made perfect in weakness." So, I will boast all the more gladly of my weaknesses, so that the power of Christ may dwell in me. Therefore I am content with weaknesses, insults, hardships, persecutions, and calamities for the sake of Christ; for whenever I am weak, then I am strong.

—2 Corinthians 12:7b–10

It wasn't obvious at the time, but one long, wind-struck stretch of the Camino would become one of the most spiritually honest moments of my pilgrimage. For ten kilometers, I walked alone into headwinds that refused to let up. There was no shade, no town, no sound but my own breath and the steady crunch of boots on gravel. What had once felt like a romantic idea—solitude on the open road—took on a more sober weight. Every step became an act of defiance, not against the wind, but against the temptation to stop.

The Meseta had already done its work of purgation. Over the preceding days, I had been stripped of hurry, distractions, and the illusion of spiritual self-sufficiency. That day marked a new phase. The Camino was no longer just emptying me. It was asking something more costly: a death of sorts. A surrender not only of burdens but of self.

Purgation reveals our attachments, but dying to self confronts our very identity. We begin to see how tightly we cling to the roles we play, the gifts we offer, the image we maintain—even in our spiritual lives. Releasing these is terrifying. However, it's here that deeper grace begins to take root. Not the kind that simply comforts, but the kind that transforms.

Growth rarely comes without resistance. Just as muscles strengthen by pushing against weight, the soul deepens through the very forces that oppose it. The wind that day felt like resistance incarnate, but it exposed a truth I needed to face: that my so-called weakness—the "thorn in the flesh" I had longed to be free of—was not a barrier to God. It was a doorway. Like Paul, I began to see that grace flows not in spite of our weakness, but through it. In our lack, Christ's sufficiency is made known. This is the paradox of the spiritual journey. To find life, we must lose it (Matthew 10:39). To walk in the power of God, we must first be emptied of ourselves.

That evening, after a day of isolation and inner wrestling, grace met me again in laughter, shared bread, and the welcome of fellow pilgrims. A simple dinner with a Camino friend and an invitation to conversation from a group of young Americans showed that I didn't know how much I had needed the gift of being received until it was offered. The wind had opposed me all day, but it led me exactly where I needed to be. This is the rhythm of grace: It meets us in resistance, strips us down to love's essentials, and then surprises us with joy.

Reflection Questions:

1. What part of your identity is hardest to surrender to God?
2. Where have you experienced purgation—and where might God be inviting you to deeper surrender?
3. How might your "thorn" become not just something to endure, but a place where grace meets you?

God of the headwind and the quiet evening, thank you for using both resistance and rest to draw me closer. Teach me not just to let go, but to lay down. Help me see my weakness not as failure, but as the sacred place where your power is made perfect.

Amen.

DAY 23

Astorga

Today has truly been a great day. I woke up late and moved at a leisurely pace, promising myself I'd stay at my next stop, Astorga, even if time allowed me to go further. So, my journey today was a more relaxed sixteen kilometers, or about ten miles. It felt refreshing to take things slowly for a change. In the second village I came to, Santibáñez de Valdeiglesias, I ran into Edwina (Ed). It had been a few days since we last saw each other, so it was nice to catch up over a cup of café con leche. Just having a quiet moment with an old Camino friend felt so grounding, a reminder of the connections we form along the way.

As we continued, we met Hank. He had originally started the Camino by bike, cycling from the Netherlands, but his bike broke down just yesterday. Now he's walking, a perfect example of how the Camino changes our plans in unexpected ways. We ended up walking together for most of the day, sometimes side by side, sometimes just near each other, together but separate.

Along the way to Astorga, we stumbled upon a small makeshift refreshment stand next to an old, abandoned building. A young Spaniard, who has been living there for three years, was serving organic juices and homemade snacks. His mission is simple yet beautiful:

to serve the pilgrims passing through. In a stretch of the Camino that could have felt barren, this little oasis of generosity was a powerful demonstration of the kindness that has marked this journey.

We made our way to a private albergue in Astorga, which turned out to be absolutely delightful. It even had a place to soak your feet—a luxury after a long day's walk. After showers and laundry, we shared a couple of beers before I toured the cathedral here in town. Later, we had a great conversation about how we can bring the spirit of the Camino back into our everyday lives once the pilgrimage is over.

If I could bring back just one thing from this experience, it would be that spirit of kindness. Kindness comes in so many forms—in shared food, in walking together, in foot massages, in listening ears, in the respect for one another's journeys, whether personal or spiritual. Kindness seems possible here on the Camino because the community is fluid, almost amoeba-like. People come and go, and there's no sense of ownership over one another—only mutual respect. It's different from the stable, structured, hierarchical communities we often find in daily life. It reminds me of Franciscan spirituality—itinerant without attachment to one place, kindness freely given and freely received.

As I sat and reflected today, I found myself wondering: Did I come on the Camino to escape from who I am? If so, why? I love my wife and my family—but do I love my life? Is my desire for anonymity here on the Camino really a desire to be someone other than who I've become? These are the kinds of questions that arise along the journey, and though they don't always have clear answers, the journey provides the space for reflection. I'll carry them with me as I continue.

The Kindness That Rises

Then he said to them all, "If any want to become my followers, let them deny themselves and take up their cross daily and follow me. For those who want to save their life will lose it, and those who lose their life for my sake will save it. What does it profit them if they gain the whole world, but lose or forfeit themselves?"

—Luke 9:23–25

One of the paradoxes of the Christian life is that the more we die to ourselves, the more we come alive. My journal entry from this day on the Camino brings that truth into focus—not through hardship or inner turmoil, but through the slow unfolding of a day marked by kindness, simplicity, and reflection. On this particular day, I walked slowly. I let go of the inner drive to push farther and instead received the gift of leisure, of presence. Along the way, old friends reappeared. New ones emerged. Strangers offered gifts. We were "together but separate," bound not by obligation but by something freer: grace.

If I have succeeded in bringing back at least one thing from the Camino, I hope it is this spirit of kindness. The longer I reflect on it, the more I realize that kindness is not simply an emotion or a virtue we try to conjure up—it is a fruit of something deeper. True kindness, the kind that heals and holds, flows out of self-denial. It is born when we stop grasping, stop defending our egos, stop needing recognition, and instead live as those who belong to one another. This phase of the Camino was a kind of death—a letting go of control, of identity, even of comfort. In that surrender, I was freer to love than ever before. Kindness became a form of resurrection.

Years later, I see how I've tried to carry this spirit home, most often through hospitality. Whether it's sharing a meal, offering a place for guests to stay, or simply creating space for someone's story, these acts—though small—have become my way of keeping the Camino alive. They are reminders that I don't need to be on a pilgrimage trail to live as a pilgrim. The path continues in the way I listen, the way I serve, the way I give without expecting anything in return.

On the Camino, we didn't own one another. We didn't fix or manage one another. We walked, we shared, we respected. That fluid, Franciscan-like community—with its itinerant grace and open-handed love—challenges me still. Can we live like that at home? I think we can, but only if we die a little each day—die to self-importance, to fear, to the need to be seen as right or successful. Only then can kindness grow unencumbered.

Reflection Questions:

1. What moments of simple kindness have stayed with you—either received or given—and what made them so impactful?
2. What does "belonging to one another" look like in your relationships and communities? Are there places where you need to release control or expectations to allow grace to grow?
3. How might you carry the spirit of kindness into your daily routines—through hospitality, presence, generosity, or open-handed love?

Holy God, the source of all kindness and grace,
teach us to slow down and open our hearts to
the gifts around us.
Help us let go of the need to control and the desire to be seen,
so that we may live freely and love deeply.
May kindness flow from a place of true surrender and presence.
Guide us to create spaces of welcome, generosity, and peace—
wherever we are, whoever we meet.

Amen.

DAY 24

Rabanal del Camino

Today marks the beginning of the final ascent to Cruz de Ferro, the iconic cross where pilgrims traditionally lay a stone representing the burdens of life they've carried from home. I'll be staying in Rabanal del Camino tonight, a small village that hosts a monastery offering Vespers at 6:30 p.m. and Compline at 9:00 p.m. During Vespers, the monks bless the pilgrims and the stones they will carry to the cross.

Having passed the halfway point of my Camino, I continue to reflect on what of the Camino I'll carry back into my regular life. That one word, *kindness*, keeps coming to mind. I've seen it in so many forms—from the villagers who greet us with the simple, heartfelt "Buen Camino" to the fellow pilgrims who share food, wine, and conversation. It's the kindness of strangers who seem to recognize that we are all walking the same Camino, and there's an unspoken understanding of what it means to support one another along the way.

I parted ways with Hank and Ed in the morning, choosing to walk alone for the rest of the day. There was a lightness in my steps as I walked. The introspection that marked the earlier days of my pilgrimage had already been done, mostly back on the Meseta. Now, it felt like a continuation of the physical journey, a walk toward something significant yet to come. Yet even in the midst of my joy today, from time to time I found myself once again reflecting ever so briefly on my "thorn in the flesh," the inauthentic self, that part of me I'm always trying to shed, always trying to move beyond. It reminded me that dying to self isn't a one-time event but a daily process, a continual act of surrender. It's a reminder that true growth comes not from avoiding our struggles but from embracing them, learning from them, and choosing daily to let go of the parts of ourselves that no longer serve us.

Saturday night, after walking twenty-one kilometers, I arrived in Rabanal del Camino. The albergue where I stayed was peaceful and simple, run by the English confraternity. In true English style, we observed teatime around 3:00 pm. It was the perfect place to rest before the next significant step: the moment when I lay my stone at Cruz de Ferro. So many pilgrims before me have left their burdens there, walking forward with renewed purpose, and tomorrow, I will do the same.

I attended Vespers, and then later Compline. Compline felt especially intimate, with fewer people in attendance, creating a sacred atmosphere. There was a quiet beauty in the service, a sense of connection with both the monks and the pilgrims gathered there. My friend Ed was there as well and read at Vespers. When invited I came forward and presented my stone, the stone I have been carrying since the beginning of my Camino, to the monk to be blessed. On one side of the rock were written the names of my former colleague and two others who joined him in his accusations of my character. On the other side, simply the word *shame*. Tomorrow, I will lay my stone at the foot of the cross. Tomorrow, I will reflect on all that it represents. Tomorrow, I will continue my walk with my heart a little lighter, knowing that forgiveness and surrender are two of the gifts I have experienced on this journey.

A Stone and a Prayer

He came out and went, as was his custom, to the Mount of Olives; and the disciples followed him. When he reached the place, he said to them, "Pray that you may not come into the time of trial." Then he withdrew from them about a stone's throw, knelt down, and prayed, "Father, if you are willing, remove this cup from me; yet, not my will but yours be done." [Then an angel from heaven appeared to him and gave him strength.]

—Luke 22:39–43

I didn't expect that the night before I reached Cruz de Ferro would be as powerful as it was for me. I had always imagined the letting go would take place at the summit itself, at the foot of that towering iron cross where pilgrims leave their stones and walk away a little freer. God's grace doesn't always wait for the climax. Sometimes grace meets us in quiet, understated places—like a small church in a mountain village.

The church that held Vespers was made of stone, unadorned, worn, and beautiful in its simplicity. The service was short, and while I don't remember the exact words spoken, I do remember the moment when the monks offered a blessing, not only for us but for the stones we would carry to the cross. That surprised me. I had heard about laying down burdens at Cruz de Ferro, but I hadn't anticipated the meaningfulness of even this small act with sacred attention. Somehow, it made everything feel more intentional, more holy.

Many pilgrims carry a stone to the cross. Some pick them up along the way; others bring them from home. Mine had been in my backpack since the beginning—a small, smooth stone, tucked away but never far from reach. I had held it in moments of prayer, squeezed it in frustration, and touched it instinctively when I needed strength. It had become, almost without my noticing, a symbol of all I was carrying within.

What struck me about the blessing was how ordinary it was. There were no dramatic gestures, no elaborate rituals—just a quiet prayer that God would use what we carried, for the purpose God intended. That's the heart of any true blessing, I think. It's not about changing the object itself but about reorienting our relationship to it. A blessing turns something mundane into something sacred. It opens us to God's intention.

Until that evening, I had thought of my stone primarily as a burden to be rid of. Through the act of blessing, I began to understand it differently. This wasn't about discarding something unpleasant; it was about surrendering it to God. Surrender isn't forgetting. Forgiveness isn't denial. Both are acts of trust—placing something into God's hands and asking God not to erase it, but to redeem it.

In a way, that night's prayer echoed the one Jesus prayed in Gethsemane: "Not my will but yours be done." It was a moment of letting go, not with certainty, but with faith. I didn't need to explain what the stone represented. God already knew. The blessing wasn't a solution; it was a sacrament—a physical, visible sign that grace had already begun its work. When I found myself at the foot of the cross the next day, the stone was already lighter in my pack. Because my soul was lighter too.

Reflection Questions:

1. What burden have you been carrying that might be ready for surrender, not as a rejection, but as a trust-filled offering to God?
2. What does it mean to you to bless something—to ask that God use it for his purpose, even if it's broken or painful?
3. Can you recall a time when you realized grace was already at work before you even asked for it?

Gracious God,
you know the weight I carry,
even when I cannot name it.
You see the prayers hidden in my heart,
the burdens I carry,
the hopes I dare not speak aloud.
Teach me to surrender—not to forget, but to trust.
Bless what I bring to you,
and use it for the purpose you intend.
Let grace meet me in the quiet,
and redemption rise from even the smallest offering.

Amen.

Resurrection

DAY 25

The Mountaintop

My friend Ed, a therapist from England, continues along the journey with me. Our conversations have been some of the most healing moments on this path—gentle, honest, and holy. It's incredible how God places the right people in our lives at just the right time. Who would have thought that I would have the ear of a trained therapist on the Camino, not just for an hour but for many hours? Through her presence, and others, I've experienced something akin to grace walking beside me. Walking in that grace, I have received forgiveness and, in turn, have been able to forgive others.

Leaving Rabanal del Camino, I passed a small chapel dedicated to peregrinos. I stepped inside to pray, and without warning, I wept. Not from sadness, but from an overwhelming awareness of God's presence—as though every step of the Camino had led to this moment. As I ascended the mountain, my heart was full. I wanted to walk alone, to meet this moment in solitude. Rounding a bend, I saw the tall pole of Cruz de Ferro rising into view, and joy surged within me.

But that joy soon turned into something else—grief, frustration, even anger. It's obvious I still have some spiritual work to do in conquering my judgmental spirit. In fairness to me, however, the scene at the cross felt like Disneyland. What I had anticipated to be a holy, sacred moment felt like a circus. Pilgrims were laughing, posing for photos, and taking selfies. Not to compare myself to Jesus, but in that moment, I sure could understand why he overturned the tables in the Temple court. I stood back, my rock still in my hand, and waited nearly an hour for the crowd to dissipate. I wanted to lay my stone down not in front of an audience, but in the quietness of worship.

When at last the crowds moved on, I approached the cross, and in one of the most profound moments of the Camino, I laid my stone at the foot of Jesus. A small, simple act, and yet for me, sacramental: an outward and visible sign of an inward and spiritual grace. I've known in my head for years that Christ has forgiven me, that in him my shame is taken away. This small act—this tactile laying down the weight of a stone—helped move that truth from my head into my heart. The sacrament became embodied. It became real.

As I walked down from the mountain into Molinaseca, I felt peace I hadn't known before. Not only that, but for the first time in days, I walked without pain in my legs or knees. I can feel the prayers of those back home for me, and I am deeply grateful. It was a pain-free day, and it felt like a benediction.

Now, here in Molinaseca, I'm shifting pace. Slowing down. I'll stay at this gentler rhythm to meet Pamela when she arrives. I want to be truly present with her. To hold space for her own Camino, her own journey. If I can offer her the space to experience even a fraction of the peace I feel now, it will be a gift.

In many ways, I feel like my Camino has ended at Cruz de Ferro. At least, the inner one. I'm open, of course, to what God still may want to do, but that moment marked the close of a chapter in my life. Now, the work ahead is this: Do not to pick up the rock again. As for today, I rest in God's grace.

The Cross, the Stone, and the Shame Left Behind

So if anyone is in Christ, there is a new creation: everything old has passed away; see, everything has become new! All this is from God, who reconciled us to himself through Christ, and has given us the ministry of reconciliation; that is, in Christ God was reconciling the world to himself, not counting their trespasses against them, and entrusting the message of reconciliation to us. So we are ambassadors for Christ, since God is making his appeal through us; we entreat you on behalf of Christ, be reconciled to God.

—2 Corinthians 5:17–20

I now see how much I carried to Cruz de Ferro—not just physically but spiritually. I had believed something sacred would happen there. I prayed toward it, anticipated it, even prepared for it. Strangely, despite my anticipation, when it did happen—when grace actually showed up, I was caught off guard.

It reminds me of that desperate father in Mark 9, pleading for his son's healing. When Jesus tells him that all things are possible for one who believes, the man cries out, "I believe; help my unbelief!" That paradox has always stayed with me. On my walk up the mountain, I believed something would happen at the cross. Still, as I approached, rock in hand, part of me doubted. Could such a simple act truly shift something as heavy as shame?

The day had already been filled with grace. In Rabanal del Camino the night before, the monks had blessed the pilgrims—and the stones we carried. It struck me as odd at first, blessing a burden. Then again, a blessing is simply a prayer that God would use what is being blessed for God's holy purpose. That blessing lingered with me as I climbed, alone, heart full, longing for something real.

When I placed my stone, something happened. It wasn't dramatic, but it was unmistakable. What I had long known in my head—that in Christ I am a new creation—sank deeper into my heart.

I recently rediscovered the photo of the rock I carried to the cross. I shared the photo with a friend. I told her that I remembered writing people's names on one side, but I'd completely forgotten writing the word *shame* on the other. When she saw it, she said simply, "Well, it appears you truly laid down your shame at the cross." Her words undid me. I hadn't just left a stone behind—I had left shame behind, and by God's grace, I've never picked it back up. I had become a new creation.

That evening, I walked into Molinaseca without pain, for the first time in days. It felt like a benediction. Though the physical Camino continued, my inner Camino—at least that chapter—felt complete. I still believe. Even now, when my belief falters, God continues to meet me in my unbelief—with grace enough for both.

Reflection Questions:

1. What burdens—emotional, spiritual, or relational—are you still carrying that Christ has already invited you to lay down?
2. In what ways have you experienced God's healing through the presence and listening ear of another person?
3. Are there moments in your life when you've said, "I believe; help my unbelief"? How did God respond to that vulnerability?

Gracious God,
you meet me in the places I least expect
—with mercy for my pain and grace for my unbelief.
Thank you for the strength to carry what needed carrying,
and the grace to finally let it go.
Help me not to take back what I've laid at your feet.
Teach me to trust that your healing is real
—even when it arrives quietly.
When I waver, remind me that your grace is always enough,
for my belief, and for my unbelief.

Amen.

DAY 26

Ponferrada Pause

Last night brought a sweet and simple farewell dinner with Ed and Patrick: just fruit, cheese, and bread. Humble and satisfying, fitting for the Camino. We said our goodbyes to Ed, who's been a steady and healing presence on the journey. These Camino goodbyes are always layered—sadness, gratitude, and a deep sense that we've shared something sacred, even if only for a few days. Rather than following my normal routine in Ponferrada of finding an albergue on my arrival, I had already booked a hotel and decided to take a pause, to slow down and breathe a little deeper. It's a rhythm I'm learning—movement and rest, solitude and community.

In town, there's a Templar castle, which now houses a museum that I had hoped to visit, but it's closed on Mondays. Still, the respite in my journey wasn't in vain. As a treat to myself, I had all my laundry done—a luxury on the Camino that feels as indulgent as a spa day anywhere else. After showering and dropping off my laundry, I went straight to the church for prayer. The quiet space, the flicker of candles, the beauty of the stained glass windows—it grounded me. I needed that moment of stillness.

Later in the day, I met a Jesuit priest named Tony, who's also walking the Camino. We grabbed beers and shared stories. Tony has lived a life that sounds like a novel: He lives in Moscow and serves as the provincial for all Jesuits in the region of the former Soviet Union. That means he oversees the entire Jesuit mission there—a role he assumed after the mysterious death of his predecessor.

Before serving as the provincial in Moscow, he served in Siberia. Father Tony originally hailed from Richardson, Texas, and we discovered we shared more in common than expected, and our connection was almost immediate. He's also friends with my Roman Catholic companions, Maura and Mary, whom I hadn't seen in about two weeks. The conversations have been rich and meaningful—God has truly blessed me with companions whose presence has been both comforting and transformative.

At one point during our conversation, I looked up—and there was Maura walking toward us with her daughter Mary. This "chance" meeting felt like an unexpected family reunion. Maura and Mary were accompanied by a father and son duo from Italy—Massimo and Matteo. After short pleasantries, we made our way through the town square to Mass at the main church, five Roman Catholics and an Episcopalian. It was one of those Camino moments: unplanned, full of connection and surprise.

After Mass, we wandered to the main square where the whole town was celebrating a soccer championship. The energy was infectious, flags waving, drums beating, and laughter echoing off the buildings. Later in the evening, I joined a group of fellow peregrinos for beers—a wonderfully international bunch: Danish, Finnish, German, Australian, an American from Philadelphia, and me.

All in all, it was a great day—a much-needed mix of rest, reconnection, and reflection. Slowing down feels right. I sense I'm entering the final movement of this long walk, and I want to be attentive to what's left to see, to hear, to receive. The mountain has been climbed. Now comes the descent—gentler, perhaps, but no less holy. As I lay in my hotel room, I entertain the thought once again that each step taken brings me that much closer to Pamela's arrival in Sarria.

The Gift of the Pause

Then the word of the LORD came to him, saying, "What are you doing here, Elijah?" He answered, "I have been very zealous for the LORD. . . . I alone am left, and they are seeking my life, to take it away." He said, "Go out and stand on the mountain before the LORD, for the LORD is about to pass by." Now there was a great wind . . . but the LORD was not in the wind; and after the wind an earthquake, but the LORD was not in the earthquake; and after the earthquake a fire, but the LORD was not in the fire; and after the fire a sound of sheer silence. When Elijah heard it, he wrapped his face in his mantle and went out and stood at the entrance of the cave.

—1 Kings 19:9b–13

There are moments on pilgrimage—just as in life—when the holiest thing we can do is stop. Not for weakness or weariness alone, but because the Spirit invites us into stillness. Into the midst of that pause, God came. I had embraced stillness many times along the Camino. In the wide silence of the Meseta. In solitary walks. In empty churches and hushed mornings. Much of what I encountered in those pauses was pain, doubt, and the ache of old wounds rising to the surface.

Stillness had served its purpose, but it had not always been comforting. What made this pause different was that, for the first time, I heard something else. I heard grace. I felt the gentle emergence of joy. The silence hadn't changed—but what the silence held had. I was no longer listening from a place of hurt and pain, but from the freedom that follows surrender.

That day, over lunch in a quiet café, I met with Father Tony. Unexpectedly, I told him I was a priest. That may sound small, but until that moment—except for one early slip with Maura and Mary—I hadn't told anyone on the Camino that I was an Episcopal priest. Too much of my identity had been wrapped in hurt, shame, and vocational uncertainty. I'd carried it silently, unsure if I could still claim it aloud. Something had changed at Cruz de Ferro. I didn't just lay down a stone; I laid down the fear that saying who I was might somehow undo me.

Telling Tony wasn't a performance or a résumé drop. It was quite natural, true. In that moment, I realized I no longer felt the need to defend or hide my calling. I wasn't explaining. I was simply being a priest, walking the Camino, listening for the voice of God. The day had begun in solitude and ended in celebration, and somewhere in the middle, I remembered who I was.

We often imagine resurrection as something loud and unmistakable. The risen Christ, however, chose to come quietly—to a garden, to a beach, to a hidden road. Resurrection doesn't always shout. Sometimes it simply comes in the quiet like it did for Elijah and invites us to speak our own name again. In Ponferrada, I did.

The descent from Cruz de Ferro had begun—not into darkness, but into return. I was no longer descending depleted. I was descending full. Full of peace, of memories, of a name I no longer feared to claim, Father Kevin.

Reflection Questions:

1. What part of your identity have you kept hidden out of fear or shame? What would it mean to speak it again with trust?
2. How have unexpected companions reminded you of who you are in Christ?
3. Is there a quiet joy or calling in your life that God might be inviting you to reclaim?

God of holy pause,
you meet us not only in the sacred spaces we expect,
but in the quiet corners of ordinary days.
Thank you for stillness that restores,
and companions who help us speak the truth about who we are.
Help me to listen for your voice in rest as well as in motion.
Teach me to trust what you've healed,
to claim what you've redeemed,
and to walk forward without fear—
not because I'm strong, but because you are.

Amen.

DAY 27

The Heat, the Heart, and a Jesuit from Texas

Today's walk was a different kind of challenge. The temperature soared to 102 degrees Fahrenheit, and the last nine kilometers were uphill and relentless. My original plan was to stop in Cacabelos, but when I learned that Tony, Maura, and Mary were pressing on to Villafranca del Bierzo, I knew I wanted to be with them. So, I pushed forward, legs aching, the heat searing and oppressive—but my spirits lifted by the thought of their company.

That afternoon, we found a shaded table and shared beers and conversation. Later, Jordan joined us. Since Maura and Tony already knew I was a priest, I decided to share that information with Jordan as well. He was genuinely surprised—in a good way—and what followed was the kind of theological conversation I've been craving this whole journey. We talked about the Camino and how, despite being walked by thousands, deep conversations about faith, meaning, and mystery along its way are surprisingly rare. We wondered aloud why that is. Why aren't such spaces for honesty and depth more common?

Later, we all went to Mass at a convent then gathered for dinner—a simple but beautiful spaghetti and salad meal prepared by Massimo,

Matteo's father. It reminded me again how profound the simplest gestures can be. Hospitality, conversation, shared bread—these are the sacraments of the road. Over dinner, Tony shared a story I'll never forget.

In one of the satellite countries of the former Soviet Union populated with many people of the Islamic faith, he met a Christian man who had waited over sixty years to receive Holy Communion. The last priest to visit his village had come in 1941, before Stalin's purges swept through the country. This man prayed every single day for a priest to return. When Tony arrived years later, he assumed the man would need preparation for receiving the sacraments since there had not been a priest in the village for more than sixty years, but the man assured Father Tony he was ready. Spiritually prepared, steady, faithful.

A Muslim friend of the man approached Father Tony to offer testimony to the man's readiness. He told Father Tony that the man in question was a righteous man. He told him that his arrival in the village after sixty years was nothing short of an answer to his friend's decades of prayer. Then he said, "We both worship the one true God." That story stopped me in my tracks. In that man's patience and devotion, and in his friend's witness across the boundaries of faith, was something holy—something pure. A reminder that faith, when lived humbly and deeply, reaches across boundaries and outlasts oppression.

This journey continues to open my heart in ways I didn't expect. It reaches across our boundaries of denominations and, in this case, expressions of faith. As I reflect tonight on today's events, I'm reminded again that the Camino is less about reaching Santiago, and more about walking with open eyes and ears and hearts, ready to receive grace in all its surprising forms.

Other Sheep, One Shepherd

For thus says the LORD: To the eunuchs who keep my sabbaths, who choose the things that please me and hold fast my covenant, I will give, in my house and within my walls, a monument and a name better than sons and daughters; I will give them an everlasting name that shall not be cut off. And the foreigners who join themselves to the LORD, to minister to him, to love the name of the LORD, and to be his servants . . . these I will bring to my holy mountain, and make them joyful in my house of prayer . . . for my house shall be called a house of prayer for all peoples.

—Isaiah 56:4–7

One of the paradoxes of pilgrimage is how it draws together seekers from every imaginable background—and yet deep spiritual conversations often remain rare. Many people walk with quiet intentions, carrying questions too tender to voice or wounds too deep to share. So, when moments of honest, searching dialogue appear, they feel like holy ground.

That's what happened on that day. The gift was not only in the conversation, but in what it revealed: The more deeply rooted we are in our own faith, the more open we become to hearing how God is at work outside our tradition. True conviction does not require defensiveness; it grants freedom. It makes room.

It is a mistake to believe that openness means compromise. In truth, openness is often the fruit of maturity—an awareness that God is bigger than the boundaries we draw. When we are secure in our own identity as beloved children of God, we no longer have to be suspicious of someone else's story. We can listen with curiosity instead of fear.

Isaiah's prophetic vision expands the frame: a house of prayer for all peoples. A faith that welcomes the foreigner, the outsider, the one who was once assumed to be beyond the circle. This isn't relativism—it's reverence. Reverence for a God whose mercy exceeds our maps, and whose Spirit blows where it will.

I found myself reminded of Jesus' words in John's Gospel: "I have other sheep that do not belong to this fold." In its context, this verse referred to those outside the Jewish faith, but does God's grace end there? There is mystery here—divine inclusion that challenges our categories and stretches our comfort. It doesn't erase distinctiveness; it honors it. It insists that grace is not the exclusive property of any one group, denomination, or tradition.

The Gospel, like the Camino, invites us to draw wider circles of inclusion. To listen. To receive. To bless. To believe that sometimes the clearest echoes of God's voice come not from within the fold, but from its edges—where the Spirit is already at work, waiting for us to notice.

Reflection Questions:

1. Are there voices outside your tradition that have helped you hear or understand God more clearly? How did you respond?
2. What boundaries—denominational, theological, or cultural—do you find yourself clinging to out of fear rather than faith?
3. How might you practice drawing wider circles of welcome in your life of faith, as Isaiah and Jesus both envision?

God of all sheep who hear your voice,
you are not confined by our borders,
nor contained by our understanding.
You move through unfamiliar paths
and speak through unexpected voices.
Thank you for the grace that grounds us—
grace that frees us from fear
and opens us to your wide mercy.
Give me the courage to listen with love,
to welcome without condition,
and to recognize you in those I least expect.
Let my life be a house of prayer for all people,
and may your Spirit lead me wherever love is needed most.

Amen.

DAY 28

The Last Mountain and Last Goodbyes

I'm now in O Cebreiro—perched atop the final mountain range of the Camino. The climb today was long and grueling, and while it wasn't quite as punishing as the Pyrenees, it still took a toll. My knees are screaming at me tonight, and I'm looking forward to the relief of Aleve before bed. Despite the physical challenge, there's something incredibly satisfying about reaching this place. From here, Santiago feels not just close, but real.

Earlier today, I passed through Trabadelo, where I stopped for breakfast and ran into Barbara, Jordan's mother. She and I had a lovely conversation about the spiritual side of the Camino—or, sometimes, the frustrating absence of it. She told me how much she appreciated the discussion her son Jordan and I had shared with Father Tony and Maura the previous day. It meant a lot to hear that. Since Cruz de Ferro, I've slowly started sharing with selected companions that I'm a priest. It's led to some unexpected and beautiful conversations, especially with those who've been longing for something deeper on this journey.

Maura and I walked part of the day together as well. I spoke a little about my doctor of ministry studies, and she—ever the thoughtful and curious soul—listened with real engagement. She's deeply Roman Catholic and embodies that classic definition of theology offered by Saint Anselm: faith seeking understanding. Conversations with her feel like shared mental hikes—challenging and edifying in the best way.

The reality is, tomorrow will probably be the last day I travel with these friends. I'll be slowing my pace in an effort to time my arrival in Sarria to meet Pamela, and that means letting go of the rhythm I've found with this group. It's bittersweet. These last few days—filled with theological conversation, shared meals, and quiet Masses—have been incredibly meaningful. I hope to see Father Tony for dinner tonight, and we're all planning to meet up for breakfast tomorrow, and then our paths will likely diverge.

Still, I leave this little mountain village with a full heart. The Camino has given me more than I could've asked for—in beauty, in companionship, in moments of grace. Though my legs are tired, and the end of the journey is near, my spirit feels stronger than ever.

That's the Deal

"This is my commandment, that you love one another as I have loved you. No one has greater love than this, to lay down one's life for one's friends. You are my friends if you do what I command you. I do not call you servants any longer, because the servant does not know what the master is doing; but I have called you friends, because I have made known to you everything that I have heard from my Father. You did not choose me but I chose you. And I appointed you to go and bear

fruit, fruit that will last, so that the Father will give you whatever you ask him in my name. I am giving you these commands so that you may love one another."

—John 15:12–17

O Cebreiro marked the last mountain before the descent into Santiago. It also marked the end of a particular rhythm I had come to cherish, and I knew that once I slowed my pace I would be walking alone again, at least for a while, as most of the friends I had come to treasure would continue on without me.

I left the village with a full heart, but I also left with the ache of goodbye. It's something pilgrims rarely talk about—the way the Camino opens your heart and then, again and again, invites you to let go. People enter your life in unexpected ways, walk with you for a stretch, and then—just as suddenly—are gone.

I've come to see that day as a sacred threshold. A moment when joy and grief held hands. It reminded me of a line from the movie *Shadowlands* where Anthony Hopkins, portraying C. S. Lewis, reflects on his wife's death, saying: "The pain now is part of the happiness then. That's the deal." We grieve only because something beautiful has been lost—and it was beautiful because it was real.

I've seen that truth in many places since. Most tenderly in the season of caring for my aging parents—my mother for seven months, my father for two years. Those days brought deep joy: the intimacy of caring, the gift of time. The grief that followed was equally profound. That's the deal. To love well is to grieve deeply. I wouldn't trade the sorrow, because it testifies to what was good and holy about those days ministering to their needs.

O Cebreiro was one of those places where something ended, and something else quietly began. My own healing was making room for someone else's. The Camino was no longer only about what I needed. It was becoming something shared.

Scripture is full of such turning points—transfigurations, farewells, descents from mountains. After his transfiguration on the mountaintop, Jesus did not remain in glory; he descended toward Jerusalem, toward the cross, toward the ultimate act of love. "Greater love has no one than this," he said, "to lay down one's life for one's friends" (John 15:13, NIV). Thresholds like these don't always feel like progress, but they are sacred spaces—where clarity comes not in the light alone, but in the willingness to walk down into the shadowed valleys for the sake of others. On the Camino, and in life, God meets us not only in our summits but in our surrender. In our goodbyes, our griefs, and our letting go, we are reminded that love often looks like sacrifice—and that even in descent, we are held in grace.

Reflection Questions:

1. Where in your life have you felt the sorrow of a meaningful goodbye?
2. How have joy and grief been intertwined in your story?
3. What have you learned from the pain that followed beauty?

God of every season,
you give us moments of deep joy
and the ache that follows when they pass.
Teach us to receive both as sacred,
to honor the letting go as much as the receiving.
At each threshold, remind us that we are held.
Let our grief be a sign of our love,
and let our love be a glimpse of your grace.

Amen.

DAY 29

Settling into Stillness

Today's walk was beautiful. From O Cebreiro, the climb to Alto do Poio—the highest point of the Camino—was tougher than I'd anticipated. Reaching the summit brought a sense of peace, and the descent was lovely. After my initial climb, the trail led mostly downhill through the lush green hills of Galicia, a region that's come alive with color and quiet charm. We followed the river down into the town of Triacastela, a soothing rhythm of water gently flowing by and then occasionally pouring over small waterfalls.

I spent the day walking with Maura. We've had some truly meaningful conversations about spouses, children, faith, and the surprising ways God's goodness shows up in our lives. She's been a grounding presence on this journey—intelligent, compassionate, and full of spiritual depth.

Walking with us are Massimo and Matteo, the Italian father and son who've also become part of this small, unexpected Camino *comunidad.* Matteo's love for Scripture is palpable, and his youthful enthusiasm blends well with his father's more grounded, fatherly wisdom. Alongside Barbara and Jordan, these friends have formed a kind of spiritual community for me—one I didn't know I needed, but now deeply treasure.

This morning, I had to say goodbye to Father Tony over breakfast, where we all gathered before setting out. It was harder than I expected. Our conversations over the last few days have meant so much—conversations that were theological, personal, and vulnerable. His witness has deeply impacted me. I've been blessed by the friendships God has orchestrated on this pilgrimage.

I've arrived in Triacastela, the last leg of my journey before meeting Pamela in Sarria on Monday. That means it's time to really slow my pace—something that's not always easy on the Camino but feels right for this moment. I checked into a municipal albergue that, frankly, looked like it might be a disaster at first glance—but turned out to be just fine. That evening, I went to Mass again with Maura. The priest was incredibly welcoming and clearly passionate about making the non-religious pilgrims feel at home. He led the service informally, gathering us around the altar, sprinkling in humor and reflection as he went. It felt accessible and sacred all at once.

Earlier in the day, we passed through Fonfría, where we had crepes. It was one of those small but perfect Camino moments—laughter, warm food, and rest before continuing on. And it was followed by an evening of more food, wine, and soccer.

Tomorrow, I'll walk a short ten kilometers to Samos, home to Spain's oldest and largest Benedictine monastery. I'm hoping to stay there overnight and enter into the rhythm of liturgical prayer with the monks. Even with that extended stay, I'll still arrive in Sarria a day early, which means I may need to check into a hotel since albergues typically only allow you to stay one night. It's a friendly reminder that you're on pilgrimage, not on vacation, but that's a small inconvenience.

God hasn't been speaking to me in dramatic ways lately—not like God did back in the Meseta or at Cruz de Ferro—but I'm walking in a quiet joy now. It's as if God is confirming with each step on this side of Cruz de Ferro that something powerful within me truly happened at the cross. Ever since that day, I've been filled with a joy that comes from God's presence in community, in beauty, in shared meals, and in simple, sacred moments.

Like a River, Gently Now

Jesus answered her, "If you knew the gift of God, and who it is that is saying to you, 'Give me a drink,' you would have asked him, and he would have given you living water." The woman said to him, "Sir, you have no bucket, and the well is deep. Where do you get that living water? Are you greater than our ancestor Jacob, who gave us the well, and with his sons and his flocks drank from it?" Jesus said to her, "Everyone who drinks of this water will be thirsty again, but those who drink of the water that I will give them will never be thirsty. The water that I will give will become in them a spring of water gushing up to eternal life."

—John 4:10–14

After the dramatic release at Cruz de Ferro and the long, emotional climb to O Cebreiro, the next stage of the Camino introduced something different—stillness. The stream that flowed through this part of the Camino became a mirror of my inner life. The first stages of the Camino felt like rapids—emotionally intense, full of questions and spiritual wrestling. Now, my spirit had begun to move at a gentler pace. Something had settled. Not because all the answers had come, but because I no longer needed them to keep walking. I thought of the difference between a wadi—a creek bed that is dry except in the rainy season—and a spring-fed stream that flows always. God's presence, I was learning, is less like a flash flood and more like an underground spring: steady, sustaining, unseen but real. Jesus uses this same imagery to describe the living water that he gives to those who follow him.

I realize now just how essential spiritual friendship is to faithful Christian living. It isn't simply about camaraderie or getting along—it's about being knit together in Christ, in mutual trust and vulnerability. Saint Aelred of Rievaulx wrote in his *Spirituali Amicitia* (*Spiritual Friendship*), "Since it is fitting that my friend be a guardian of our mutual love, or the guardian of my own spirit so as to preserve all its secrets in faithful silence."[5] On this day of walking, I began to understand what he meant.

True spiritual friends don't just walk beside you—they help you listen for the voice of God when your own ears grow tired. They remind you who you are when shame has clouded your memory. They speak truth gently, hold silence reverently, and share joy fully. Spiritual friends on the Camino might also be the ones to hand you a crepe, toast you with a glass of wine, or cheer with you during a soccer match.

Grace that day didn't arrive in thunder or vision. It arrived in the feeling of the trail softening beneath my feet. God was there—in the stream, in the silence, and in the friendships that flowed with me

---

5. Aelred of Rievaulx, *Spiritual Friendship* (Cistercian Publications, 1977), 55.

toward Santiago. Some days, pilgrimage is fire. Other days, it is a river, and in both, God flows faithfully with us.

Reflection Questions:

1. Where in your life have you experienced God's presence, not in dramatic revelation but in quiet joy and stillness? How did that shape your understanding of how God speaks?
2. What friendships in your life have drawn you closer to God? Who has walked beside you like Maura, offering spiritual depth and simple companionship?
3. What might it look like for you to slow your pace—physically, emotionally, or spiritually? Are there parts of your life that need a more contemplative rhythm?

God of quiet joy and gentle presence,
Thank you for walking beside me
even when I do not hear you loudly.
Help me to slow my steps
and open my heart to the sacred that surrounds me—
in rivers that flow, in friends who listen,
in sacred conversations, and in stillness that settles the soul.
Let me receive your grace not only in fire, but also in laughter,
not only in struggle, but also in shared bread and sacred silence.

Amen.

DAY 30

Parting and Peace in Aguiada

After touring the breathtaking monastery at Samos, I had originally planned to spend the night there, soaking in the beauty and entering into the rhythm of monastic prayer. Saying goodbye to Maura and Mary proved harder than I expected. When we parted ways after one last café con leche together, I found myself emotional—tears came more easily than I thought they would.

I didn't feel like staying in Samos after that. The monastery, as magnificent as it was, suddenly felt a bit empty without them. So, I laced up my boots and started walking again, carrying not just my backpack, but a quiet ache of departure. The trail wound through a serene oak forest, with a cool stream trickling alongside. It was peaceful and beautiful—almost idyllic—though my twenty-five-pound pack made sure I didn't romanticize it too much.

I stopped about five kilometers shy of Sarria, where I'm meeting Pamela on Monday. I wanted to give myself space to rest and reflect before her arrival and not spend every night in one place. I found a small albergue in the village of Aguiada—a lovely, quiet spot that turned out to be exactly what I needed. Dinner that night was a traditional Galician meal. We had a delicious lentil-based soup, fish empanadas, quiche Lorraine, salad, bread, and local wine. Dessert was the regional *Tarta de Santiago* (almond cake) with fresh fruit, followed by a potent local liqueur café that warmed me from the inside out.

Later that evening, the albergue patio came alive. A Korean woman and a French pilgrim picked up a guitar and began to play and sing. Soon, others joined. Someone found a piano, and before long, we were dancing under the stars—laughter echoing through the night like an impromptu blessing. It reminded me, once again, of how joy is found in the simplest of things: music, shared meals, and community. Tomorrow, I'll walk the final stretch into Sarria, maybe get a haircut—if I can find a barber who understands "just a little off the top." I don't have much to spare!

The Dance of the Trinity

"I ask not only on behalf of these, but also on behalf of those who will believe in me through their word, that they may all be one. As you, Father, are in me and I am in you, may they also be in us, so that the world may believe that you have sent me. The glory that you have given me I have given them, so that they may be one, as we are one, I in them and you in me, that they may become completely one, so that the world may know that you have sent me and have loved them even as you have loved me."

—John 17:20–23

As I reflect on that night, filled with camaraderie, I'm reminded of words once spoken by one of my seminary professors: "The Christian life is sharing in and showing forth the triune life of God." There's an ancient word used by the early Church fathers to give definition to the way the Trinity relates; *perichoresis*—a Greek term meaning "mutual indwelling" or "the dance around." *Choresis* is where we derive the word "choreography." For early theologians, it was the most beautiful image they could find to describe how Father, Son, and Spirit exist in joyful, loving movement with one another. Each distinct, yet united. Each giving, receiving, and making room for the other. The love between them is not static but flowing, dynamic—a divine communion of delight.

On that patio, under the stars of rural Galicia, we pilgrims mirrored that mystery in our own imperfect way. We moved together, gave space, shared laughter, and offered presence. We entered a rhythm that was older than us and larger than us—a rhythm that felt, somehow, sacred. This, too, is part of pilgrimage. Not just the miles walked, or the prayers whispered, but the surprising, Spirit-led moments when joy bursts forth, unbidden and full of grace. These are not distractions from the journey. They are the journey—the human echo of divine life. That night in Aguiada reminded me that the Christian life is not only about sacrifice and solitude. It is also about joy. About making room. About dancing with others in the generous love of God.

Reflection Questions:

1. When have you experienced unexpected joy that felt like a gift from God?
2. How does community and shared joy reflect the nature of the Trinity?

3. In what ways might you be invited into the "dance" of divine life today?

Holy God,
Father, Son, and Holy Spirit:
Creator, Redeemer, Sustainer.
You are joy, peace, and love.
Thank you for the moments of laughter
that remind us we are not alone,
for strangers who become friends,
and for the sacred beauty of shared life.
Teach us to live in rhythm with your Spirit—
to give, to receive, and to dance in God's
love with one another.

Amen.

DAY 31

A Rainy Morning, a Full Heart in Sarria

I woke up late this morning. Everyone else in the room had already packed up and left, but I wasn't in any hurry. It was lightly raining, and I wasn't exactly eager to get started. I puttered around a bit, sipping coffee and waiting for the weather to ease up. Eventually, the rain let up to a light drizzle, so I set off for my short walk—just four kilometers into Sarria, where I'll wait a couple of days for Pamela to arrive.

Once I arrived in town, I wandered up the Camino in search of breakfast and café con leche. After finishing, I asked the café owner—in my best Spanglish—if he knew of a cheap room for a couple of nights. I wanted something a little more private than an albergue, knowing that Pamela would appreciate a quieter space.

The next thing I knew, a worker at the café had his car in the street with both passenger doors open. He motioned for me to throw my bag in the back seat and my butt in the front seat. Without hesitation, I did as he commanded while wondering if my family would ever see me again. He drove me back down the street to a bar/hotel, where

I now have a private room and a shared bath. A total blessing. God is good.

Later in the day, I wandered into a bookstore, and who should I see walking by but Father Tony. He's now traveling with an old college friend and that friend's family. His friend teaches philosophy at Boston College, and his wife, who's from Belgium, teaches comparative theology—specifically Christian and Hindu traditions—at the same university. Naturally, our conversation turned to Trappist beer since she was from Belgium and I'm a home brewer.

After heading back to my room, I leaned out the window to take in the afternoon breeze and saw Kim and her son Scott from California. I shouted at them, and they immediately looked up with big smiles. They were the last of my Camino friends still behind me, and I had been hoping I might see them one last time. Turns out, they'd been hoping for the same thing. We shared a beer, laughed a lot, and later that evening, had dinner together since they're also staying in Sarria tonight.

It feels like one stage of my Camino is now complete, and a new one—the final chapter, to be shared with Pamela—is about to begin. Tomorrow I'll do a few errands: scope out the hotel where Pamela and I will stay, maybe do a load of laundry, and check the bus schedules to and from Lugo. It looks like I can catch an 8:45 a.m. bus to Lugo and meet Pamela there before riding back together around 1:00 p.m. I can hardly wait—she should be landing in Madrid as I write this.

The Grace of the Threshold

The apostles gathered around Jesus, and told him all that they had done and taught. He said to them, "Come away to a deserted place all by yourselves and rest a while." For many were coming and going, and they had no leisure even to eat. And they went away in the boat to a deserted place by themselves. Now many saw them going and recognized them, and they hurried there on foot from all the towns and arrived ahead of them. As he went ashore, he saw a great crowd; and he had compassion for them, because they were like sheep without a shepherd; and he began to teach them many things.

—Mark 6:30–34

I realize now that rainy day in Sarria marked more than just a short leg of my pilgrimage—it marked a threshold. One chapter was closing, and another was about to begin. I woke up slowly, unbothered by the rush of early morning pilgrims. For once, I didn't feel compelled to keep pace. The drizzle outside gave me permission to linger. I sipped my coffee and waited—not out of laziness but in trust that whatever the day held, it would unfold in its time.

There's a term in Christian monasticism—*otium sanctum*, or "holy leisure." It refers to a sacred kind of rest, not idleness but an open posture toward God's grace. As we see in the passage above, even Jesus needed this time to be away. That day felt like an embodiment of *otium sanctum*. I wasn't striving or planning; I was simply available. Into that space of holy leisure, God poured small miracles.

I'll admit, I'm not naturally good at holy leisure. I'm more fluent in movement than stillness. Years of ministry—shaped by a Protestant work ethic and an often-unspoken pressure to "climb the ladder" of influence—trained me to equate worth with output. We wouldn't call it a corporate ladder in the Church, of course, but the impulse is the same. That's part of why the professional wound hurt so deeply—it jeopardized the trajectory I thought I needed to justify my calling. Here I was in this moment, in a quiet town, doing nothing "productive," and somehow feeling more whole than I had in years. None of this was planned, but all of it felt stitched together by something beyond coincidence.

Pilgrimage teaches us to walk with intention. It also teaches us to rest with openness. In Sarria, I learned that waiting can be holy, and that joy can find us when we stop trying to manufacture it. It arrives through strangers, old friends, and the quiet peace of being exactly where we need to be.

Reflection Questions:

1. What does "holy leisure" look like in your own life? Are there spaces where you resist resting because of internal pressure to be productive?

2. What thresholds or transitions are you standing on today? How might God be inviting you to slow down and be present in this in-between space?

3. Who are the "strangers turned companions" God has brought into your life recently? How might you be called to recognize or offer grace through them?

Gracious God,
you meet us not only in grand visions but in quiet cafés, passing conversations, and rainy mornings that slow our pace.
Teach me to trust in your timing and to welcome rest without guilt.
Soften the grip of striving in me,
and help me to receive what each moment offers—
even when I do not feel productive,
even when I do not feel in control.
Thank you for the gifts of kindness,
reconnection, and sacred thresholds.
Let me walk this day with open hands and a grateful heart.

Amen.

DAY 32

Anticipation Builds

Today was a pretty relaxed day. I started at Mesón O Tapas with a nice cup of coffee, then went to check out the hotel where Pamela and I will be staying tomorrow. Honestly, I wasn't thrilled with the location—it felt a bit too far from everything. So I inquired about a room with a private bathroom at the place I'm currently staying. Thankfully, there was availability, so I canceled the other reservation and settled into a new plan.

After a short siesta, I wandered back to Mesón O Tapas for lunch. It was there that I ran into Mona, my Camino buddy from the Netherlands. We had a nice chat over lunch, catching up on our Camino experiences and reflecting on the journey so far. She's one of the people on the Camino with whom I've had meaningful, in-depth conversations, and it was refreshing to have that connection.

I also made a trip to the local monastery to pick up a credential for Pamela—one more piece of preparation before her arrival—and checked on my laundry before meeting Mona again for dinner. Afterward, we returned to Mesón O Tapas to watch the Spain-Italy European Cup final. Spain won 4–0, clinching the championship, and the whole town seemed to erupt in celebration. There were horns honking, people singing in the streets—such a lively atmosphere!

With all the excitement going on outside, I'm hoping I'll be able to sleep tonight, but honestly, the anticipation of seeing Pamela tomorrow is overwhelming, and I'm afraid I may not sleep well. She should be in Santiago as I write this, and I can only assume the streets are exploding with jubilation there as well. She may find it hard to sleep tonight too. I'm surprising her by catching a bus to meet her in Lugo, where she is scheduled to make a transfer to Sarria in the morning. We will meet there and ride back together to Sarria. It feels like the final stage of this Camino journey is about to begin, but this time, it will be shared with Pamela. I can't wait to see her.

You Belong Here

"Do not let your hearts be troubled. Believe in God, believe also in me. In my Father's house there are many dwelling-places. If it were not so, would I have told you that I go to prepare a place for you? And if I go and prepare a place for you, I will come again and will take you to myself, so that where I am, there you may be also. And you know the way to the place where I am going." Thomas said to him, "Lord, we do not know where you are going. How can we know the way?" Jesus said to him, "I am the way, and the truth, and the life. No one comes to the Father except through me."

—John 14:1–6

That day in Sarria was about more than errands and laundry. On the surface, I was rearranging hotel reservations, picking up Pamela's pilgrim credential, and checking on clean clothes. Underneath these chores, something deeper was unfolding; I was preparing a place for someone I loved, for a shared journey, for grace to take on new form. None of these things was dramatic, but each was filled with intention.

I was offering something sacramental—an outward and visible sign of inward love and care. The simple tasks of preparation became a kind of liturgy, a way of embodying love not only in thought or speech, but in time, effort, and detail. I realized later that these were acts of love done in the language Pamela understands best.

Based on Gary Chapman's *The Five Love Languages*, Pamela's primary love language is acts of service. She doesn't need grand speeches or public declarations—she feels most loved when someone quietly lightens her load, anticipates her needs, and tends to the details that make life a little easier. That is what I was doing that day: speaking her love language. With every errand, I was quietly saying, "I see you. I've made space for you. You belong here."

It struck me how much this resembles the promise Jesus gave his disciples: "I go and prepare a place for you." Not just in some far-off heaven, but in the here and now—through love made tangible, relational, present. That kind of preparation is deeply incarnational. It mirrors the way Christ's love takes on flesh through our hands, our time, and our care for others.

Preparing a place doesn't always mean setting out fresh towels or booking a hotel room. Sometimes it looks like making time in a busy schedule for a grieving friend. Sometimes it's saving a seat for someone new in church or learning a few words of another language to welcome a neighbor. It might mean creating emotional space for a spouse or child to be fully themselves. Wherever love creates room for another soul to rest—that is sacred work.

That night, Sarria erupted with joy as Spain won the European Cup. For me, the real celebration was quieter: the anticipation of reunion, the nearness of love, and the sacred work of preparing a place, not just for Pamela, but for the final stretch of the Camino we would now walk together.

Reflection Questions:

1. Who in your life might feel most loved through practical, thoughtful service? How could you speak their love language this week?
2. What does it mean for you personally that Jesus has "gone and prepared a place" for you?
3. Where in your life is God inviting you to make space for someone new, for healing, or for grace to take root?

Christ of quiet service,
you prepare a place for us—not just in eternity,
but in every small act of love shown to us by others.
Teach me to serve with joy,
to notice the quiet needs of others,
and to prepare space for grace to dwell.
Let my hands reflect your hands,
and my heart reflect your heart.

Amen.

DAY 33

Reunion and Celebration: Pamela in Sarria

Today is the day I have been waiting for! After breakfast, I took the 9:00 a.m. bus to meet Pamela. I arrived in Lugo at 10:00 a.m., with about three hours to kill before her bus from Santiago arrived. I wandered into the Old Town, hoping to find some books in English, but without success. While walking around, I stumbled into Lugo's cathedral just as Mass had begun, so I decided to stay for the service. After Mass, I made my way back to the bus station.

There, I ran into James, a person I had met on my way to Lugo. He was an Australian living in London and working as an animator on a Disney film. By his own admission, James wasn't religious, but he loved the Camino. A few days earlier, he had stumbled into a Mass and was deeply moved by the liturgy. God truly works in mysterious ways.

Just as I sat down to enjoy my beer, Pamela texted me to let me know she had arrived in Lugo. I quickly finished my beer, but she didn't make it to the station for another fifteen minutes. When she walked off the bus, we both cried and embraced each other, feeling like it had been forever since we were last together. God couldn't have given me a better life partner—she truly is the love of my life.

We then immediately caught the bus back to Sarria, holding hands the entire way. After checking into our room and reconnecting, we went to Mesón O Tapas for lunch. We thought it would be a light meal, just a beer for me and a glass of red wine for Pamela. However, the owner, who had become a Camino friend with my numerous visits to his establishment over the last few days, in an incredible act of generosity and hospitality, brought us an entire bottle of red wine for Pamela and insisted on treating us to a bottle of white wine on the house.

Needless to say, by the time lunch was over, we were both quite relaxed, and it was a good thing we didn't have to drive. We went back to our room and ended up sleeping until around 9:15 p.m.

In the evening, we went to an Italian restaurant for dinner—this time without any wine. It had been a day of reunion, joy, and blessings, and I couldn't be happier to now be able to share this journey with Pamela.

Drawn by Beauty: Liturgy, Love, and the Light So Lovely

How lovely is your dwelling place, O Lord of hosts! My soul longs, indeed it faints for the courts of the Lord; my heart and my flesh sing for joy to the living God. Even the sparrow finds a home, and the swallow a nest for herself, where she may lay her young, at your altars, O L*ORD of hosts, my King and my God. Happy are those who live in your house, ever singing your praise. Selah*

—Psalm 84:1–4

While waiting in Lugo for Pamela's bus, I wandered into the cathedral just as Mass began. I hadn't gone looking for liturgy, but it found me. The rhythms, the gestures, the rising and falling cadence of the prayers—it all settled around me like a familiar song I didn't realize I remembered. It was simple, understated, and deeply beautiful.

One of the things that resonated with me from this day in my journal was the experience of James, who said he recently wandered into a Mass on his own. "I didn't understand it all," he admitted, "but it was . . . beautiful." That word stayed with me—*beautiful.* It brought to mind my own first experience of liturgy at the Easter Vigil years ago. The church began in total darkness. Then the Paschal candle was lit and processed into the sanctuary, flickering with promise. The Exsultet rang out, and the long arc of Scripture began to unfold—creation, covenant, deliverance, exile, longing, and then, the moment: "Alleluia, Christ is risen!" The lights blazed. The bells rang. While I didn't fully understand all that was happening, I was drawn into the divine drama anyway.

My seminary mentor—who came to the priesthood after a career in the theater—once told me, "Liturgy is sacred drama. It doesn't just tell the story of God's love; it enacts it." That day in Lugo, I saw how even someone like James, who didn't share the faith, could still be caught up in the beauty of the telling. Madeleine L'Engle once wrote: "We do not draw people to Christ by loudly discrediting what they believe . . . but by showing them a light that is so lovely that they want with all their hearts to know the source of it."[6] James felt God's presence in the liturgy, which he could not find words for. A few moments later, I too felt God's presence in my deep love for Pamela as she stepped off the bus.

We had been apart for only weeks, but the Camino had changed me. I had walked through grief, healing, surrender—and now I was ready not just to receive love again, but to make space for someone else's journey beside mine. That day, I walked into grace twice—once in a quiet cathedral, and again in a tearful embrace. Both times, it wasn't knowledge that brought me to that grace. It was beauty.

Reflection Questions:

1. Can you recall a time when beauty—not explanation—drew you closer to God? What made that experience memorable?
2. When in your life has love itself felt like worship—an embodied expression of grace or mystery?
3. Where might God be inviting you to stop striving for answers and simply step into the wonder?

---

6. Carole F. Chase, ed., *Madeleine L'Engle Herself: Reflections on a Writing Life* (WaterBrook Press, 2001), 155.

God of mystery and light,
you meet me not only in the answers, but in the awe.
Thank you for beauty that stirs the heart
before it convinces the mind—
for rituals that speak without words,
for love that enfolds without needing explanation,
and for the sacred story you continue to tell in and through my life.
Keep me open to wonder.
Draw me into the dance of your grace,
and let my life reflect a light so lovely
that others may long to know its source.

Amen.

DAY 34

A Test of Endurance and Change

We set out for Gonzar in the morning, a thirty-kilometer stretch. It was Pamela's first day of walking, and we should have chosen a shorter distance. Pamela, however, insisted on pushing through. It was a lovely walk, but the last seven kilometers were all uphill. We both had doubts about whether Pamela could make it, but she did. This section of the Camino, however, is markedly different, and I'm afraid not for the better.

With July being the traditional holiday month in Europe, the route has become packed with groups of high school students. Along with them come loud conversations and music played without headphones. At one point, after hearing one girl speak endlessly in Spanish, Pamela turned to me and said, "It's like being on the Camino with our granddaughter Lexi!" The Camino journey up to this point had been quiet and reflective; now it was noisy and chaotic.

As my frustration grew, I couldn't help but think how much this mirrors my life—full of noise and busyness, with little time given for quiet and reflection. Finally, we were able to separate ourselves from the kids. As the afternoon went on, the crowds began to thin out, and by the end of the day, I only saw one person whom I had met before Pamela joined me. This stretch of the Camino truly feels like a communal experience, and while I miss my old Camino buddies, I am incredibly blessed to be here with Pamela, my best friend.

We assumed the crowds would be staying in the major city, so we decided to push on. The uphill trek was tough, and we definitely felt the toll—my knees were sore, and Pamela's back was hurting. After such a physical effort on Pamela's part, we opted for a private albergue. It turned out to be a great choice. We had a wonderful dinner. Tonight is Pamela's first night in an albergue, and so far, she's handling it well. We are both hoping for a restful evening.

Walking Together: Love, Limits, and the Shared Camino

We who are strong ought to put up with the failings of the weak, and not to please ourselves. Each of us must please our neighbor for the good purpose of building up the neighbor. For Christ did not please himself; but, as it is written, "The insults of those who insult you have fallen on me." For whatever was written in former days was written for our instruction, so that by steadfastness and by the encouragement of the scriptures we might have hope. May the God of steadfastness and encouragement grant you to live in harmony with one another, in accordance with Christ Jesus, so that together you may with one voice glorify the God and Father of our Lord Jesus Christ.

—Romans 15:1–6

My pilgrimage had shifted in a single day. Until then, my journey had been shaped largely by solitude, punctuated by moments of companionship. I could choose my pace, set my goals, and move freely through the rhythm I had slowly come to trust: no need to hurry, no need to prove anything. That day, the rhythm changed.

Every decision now had a new layer of consideration: how far, how fast, how loud, how long. Pamela was learning the Camino in real time, without the benefit of weeks to adapt. It wasn't about weakness—she's strong and determined—but about learning how to be present with someone else's experience, not just my own. I held a tension between what I wanted and what another needed—that was the Camino now. Honestly, it's not just the Camino. It's life. It's marriage. It's ministry. It's love.

Saint Paul writes, "Let us therefore make every effort to do what leads to peace and to mutual edification . . . It is better not to do anything that will cause your brother or sister to fall" (Romans 14:19, 21, paraphrased). In Philippians 2:3–4, he urges us, "Do nothing from selfish ambition or conceit, but in humility regard others as better than yourselves. Let each of you look not to your own interests, but to the interests of others." That day, I saw how quickly I default to independence, how tempting it is to focus on what's permissible rather than what is beneficial. Not just for me, but for the one beside me. I wasn't giving up freedom. I was discovering something deeper than autonomy: communion.

The Rule of St. Benedict puts it in timeless, pastoral terms: "They should each try to be the first to show respect to the other . . . , supporting with the greatest patience one another's weaknesses of body or behavior."[7] That spirit of mutual care—of slowing down, of honoring the pace and needs of others is at the heart of any shared journey. It's not just accommodation; it's an expression of love. It's a way of saying: Your experience matters just as much as mine.

There's a holiness in an accomplishment made together. The Camino, like life, invites us to walk mindfully—not just for ourselves, but with and for each other. Love, after all, isn't just a feeling. It's a pace we agree on. It's a shared rhythm. It's choosing, every day, to walk at someone else's speed—not because we have to, but because we get to.

Reflection Questions:

1. When have you been invited to slow your pace for the sake of another? What did it teach you?
2. How do you respond to life's "crowded" seasons—when noise and disruption challenge your peace?
3. Where might you be called to mutual patience in your relationships today?

---

7. Timothy Fry, ed., *The Rule of St. Benedict in English* (Liturgical Press, 1982), 94.

Patient and gracious God,
teach me to walk not for myself alone,
but alongside those you've given me to love.
Give me the humility to slow down,
the grace to adjust my steps,
and the joy of discovering you
in the shared pace of mutual care.
May I be a gentle companion,
offering strength without control,
and love without condition.

Amen.

DAY 35

Rain, Reflection, and Realizations

This morning, after breakfast, we set out for a twenty-five-kilometer day, hoping to stop in Casanova, about the seventy-one-kilometer mark from Santiago. If all goes as planned, we should arrive in Santiago on Saturday. It rained all morning, so we walked in our ponchos, heads down and feet steady. We stopped for lunch and found a small internet café, so we thought we should send word that Pamela is alive and well, with no blisters thus far!

Today, while at lunch, who should appear at a café in Hospital Alta da Cruz but François from Ottawa. He said he didn't recognize me because I was now fit and trim and had grown a beard. I can't believe I saw him once again after a month of not seeing him. We rode the train together in France from Bayonne to Saint-Jean-Pied-de-Port. We walked the first eight kilometers to Orisson from Saint-Jean-Pied-de-Port. He tried to convince me to stay at Orisson rather than go on to Roncesvalles, but I pressed on. Just as well, it appears as if he and Danielle, the woman he was walking with, have become good friends. They walked together for two weeks, and then she went home for one week, and then rejoined him for another week. Danielle had just left to go back to France.

As we continued, the rain returned to greet us. Our original plan—well, my plan—was to walk another six kilometers to Casanova. However, with the rain falling steadily, we decided to check the availability of beds in Pontecampaña. There were only two beds left, one in one building and one in another. Not ideal. The next town on the route, Casanova, had no vacancies, so we moved on to O Coto, where we found a hotel—a Michelin 2010–rated place, no less.

A conversation with Pamela earlier in the day lingered in my mind. As a result of our conversation, it's becoming more apparent to me that my days at my parish may be numbered. I love the church deeply, but I feel constantly drained by the politics. I think my ongoing discernment around my call to my current ministry placement will be influenced by that unresolved tension. Despite the restlessness, I also had a beautiful conversation with Pamela. I told her how much my love for her and thankfulness for her have deepened during my Camino.

Listening in the Rain: The Gift of Mutual Discernment

Bear one another's burdens, and in this way you will fulfill the law of Christ. For if those who are nothing think they are something, they deceive themselves. All must test their own work; then that work, rather than their neighbor's work, will become a cause for pride. For all must carry their own loads.

—Galatians 6:2–5

Some days on pilgrimage feel more inward than outward. Rain fell for most of the day as we walked toward Casanova, keeping our heads low and our conversation sparse. Sometimes, it's precisely in those quiet, soaked hours that the most honest reflections begin to rise.

Earlier that day, a conversation with Pamela stayed with me—one of those long, slow talks that only seem to happen when the road stretches out and the usual distractions fade away. It wasn't a conversation with easy answers, but with honest questions: about calling, weariness, and the pull to something new. What surfaced in our conversation wasn't just my restlessness, but the gentle realization that I didn't have to carry it alone.

Discernment, especially around vocation, is often misunderstood as a solitary act. In the Christian tradition—and especially in communities like The Episcopal Church—calling is always confirmed in the context of community. No one discerns in a vacuum. Whether it's a call to ordained ministry, a change in life direction, or the decision to stay or go, we need the wisdom and care of others to help us hear clearly.

That day on the Camino, I was reminded that one of the greatest gifts of companionship is shared listening. Not decision-making on behalf of the other, but the willingness to wonder, to hold tension, to speak truth in love. As quoted previously, Ecclesiastes says, "For if they fall, one will lift up the other; but woe to one who is alone and falls and does not have another to help" (Ecclesiastes 4:10). I didn't fall physically that day, but something in me had been tired and uncertain for a long time.

Pamela didn't fix it; she helped lift it. That's the heart of mutual discernment. That mutual discernment was a way of living out Saint Paul's admonition to bear one another's burdens.

In Philippians 2:1–2, 4, Paul writes, "If then there is any encouragement in Christ, any consolation from love, any sharing in the Spirit . . . be of the same mind, having the same love. . . . Let each of you look not to your own interests, but to the interests of others." Discernment is not merely about what seems best for me. It's about how the Spirit speaks through love, humility, and relationship.

Sometimes the answer to a question doesn't arrive as clarity—it arrives as presence. Not every path forward will be obvious. When someone is willing to walk beside you, willing to listen without judgment or agenda, that becomes holy ground. In bearing one another's burdens, we fulfill the law of Christ.

Reflection Questions:

1. Have you ever experienced a moment of shared discernment with someone you trust? What did it reveal?

2. What voices do you invite into your discernment process? Who helps you listen for God?

3. In your own decisions—big or small—how do you balance your needs with the wisdom and care of others?

Gracious and guiding God,
thank you for those who walk beside us,
not to direct our steps, but to share in the wondering.
Help us to listen well,
to ask honest questions,
and to trust that you often speak through others.
Give us the humility to seek counsel,
and the courage to hear what we might not expect.
Let our shared journeys become sacred paths of discernment.

Amen.

DAY 36

When Tears Fall like Rain

Today, we realized why Galicia is so green—it rains constantly. We walked twenty-one kilometers in a steady downpour, our ponchos flapping with every gust of wind. The weather might have been dreary, but the beauty of the countryside more than made up for it—lush landscape and quiet lanes made this one of the most beautiful stretches we've seen since leaving Sarria. It's undeniably pastoral—rolling hills, scattered villages, and, yes, an impressive number of cows. The trail was often decorated with their . . . contributions, which added a certain earthy authenticity to the day.

Despite a rough night of sleep, we managed to meet the distance goal I had set for the day, Ribadiso de Baixo, a village about forty-four kilometers short of Santiago. We're still on track to arrive in Santiago on Saturday. Ribadiso de Baixo had come highly recommended, especially for its municipal albergue by the river, where pilgrims often soak their tired feet or even take a dip. Unfortunately, with the constant rain, that wasn't in the cards. So, we opted instead for a private albergue—comfort over charm this time.

As always, Pamela has been a trooper. Our bodies are holding up remarkably well despite—well, let's just say my "advanced" age. She, of course, is as strong and graceful as ever. During our walk, we had a lovely moment with a local farmer guiding seven or eight cattle from one field to another. Simple, pastoral beauty. These kinds of encounters seem to happen just when you need a reminder of the Camino's quiet gifts.

Pamela and I also spent much of the time talking about our lives and our future. I shared with her something that had been weighing on me—my lingering concern about some conflicts at her workplace. These conversations, though sometimes hard, are moments of grace. They deepen my gratitude for Pamela's presence on this journey—her wisdom, her patience, and her unwavering love.

As I sat here at the albergue writing, someone walked up and surprised me—Samantha from England, a fellow pilgrim I hadn't seen for a month. We embraced like old friends, and I introduced her to Pamela. I asked her where her walking partner, Maria, was. She informed me that Maria had received word that her grandmother had died, and she had chosen to walk alone in solitude for a few days. Having arrived late after a long day on the road, Samantha was hopeful that she would still be able to find a bed for the night. Another day, another stretch of the Camino behind us. Even soaked to the bone, we are surrounded by blessings.

The Ministry of Presence

When Mary came where Jesus was and saw him, she knelt at his feet and said to him, "Lord, if you had been here, my brother would not have died." When Jesus saw her weeping, and the Jews who came with her also weeping, he was greatly disturbed in spirit and deeply moved. He said, "Where have you laid him?" They said to him, "Lord, come and see." Jesus began to weep. So the Jews said, "See how he loved him!" But some of them said, "Could not he who opened the eyes of the blind man have kept this man from dying?"

—John 11:32–37

When I heard that a Camino friend had learned that her grandmother had died and decided to walk in solitude for a bit, I wasn't surprised. Grief often brings with it the need for space. Sometimes we need companionship. Sometimes we need silence. What moved me was how gently the Camino honored her choice. No judgment, no demands, just the path patiently waiting.

As a priest, I've walked with many through sorrow, and I've lived it myself. When my brother Kent died at age twenty in a motorcycle accident, I was only twenty-four. My parents were devastated. They couldn't bring themselves to choose a casket, so I did it for them. At his request, I took our grandfather to the place where Kent died. I brought the young woman who had been with Kent that night before his accident to visit my mother, so she could know what his final moments were like. Finally, I preached at the funeral—because the pastor didn't know Kent, and someone needed to speak who knew his heart.

In those moments, I wasn't offering answers; I was simply there. That's what people need in grief. Not theology. Not resolution. Just presence. Even Jesus gave us that. When Mary and Martha lost their brother Lazarus, Jesus didn't begin with a sermon or a solution. He knew resurrection was coming. He could have said, "Don't cry—I'm about to fix this." But he didn't. He wept. Out of love. Out of empathy. Because their pain mattered. That brief verse—Jesus wept—may be the most comforting in all of Scripture. It reminds us that even when we believe in resurrection, we don't have to rush past the sorrow.

What mattered most in those days wasn't theology or explanation. It was simply presence. Showing up. Doing what needed to be done. That's what I've come to believe real pastoral care is: not words, but love with flesh on it. That presence can take on many forms. I've learned that laughter is one of them. Some of the holiest moments in grief come when people begin to tell stories, especially the ones that make them laugh. They bring oxygen to the room. We don't just remember that someone died—we remember how fully they lived. That's what I hoped for Maria: that someone would walk beside her, not to fix her, but to listen. Maybe even to laugh.

I didn't know it then, but Kent's funeral became a turning point in my life. At the time, I was getting my MBA, having abandoned my earlier plans to become a Baptist minister. After the service, I walked out to find the line of family cars. My grandmother, my spiritual mentor, rolled down her window and motioned for me to come close. She didn't say much. Just, "Young man, you have missed your calling." Then she rolled the window back up.

She was right. It was through grief—my own and others'—that I found my way back to the ministry I didn't think I'd return to. Not through a vision or a voice from the heavens. Just a funeral, a faithful grandmother, and the ministry of presence.

Reflection Questions:

1. When have you been most deeply comforted by someone's presence in a time of grief—without needing them to say anything?
2. What stories—especially the funny or joyful ones—help you remember and honor someone you've lost?
3. In what ways has God used your own experience of loss to help you care for others?

God of all comfort,
teach me the sacred art of presence—
to sit with sorrow, to honor silence,
and when the time is right, to share a laugh.
Help me carry stories that heal,
and offer not explanations,
but love made visible.

Amen.

DAY 37

The Long Walk Home

A Marathon to Santiago

Are we crazy or what? We're in Santiago. We started the morning in Ribadiso de Baixo, forty-three and a half kilometers from Santiago. It was raining again, and the trail was muddy from the previous night's downpour. Our plan had been to walk to Arca, about halfway to Santiago—roughly twenty-one kilometers—rest up, and finish the journey the following day.

Something unexpected happened: We felt good. So, we kept walking. Despite a terrible night's sleep in a noisy albergue, where inconsiderate pilgrims stayed up talking well after lights went out and then crashed around early in the morning as if no one else was there, we managed to get ourselves out the door. Over breakfast, we shared our frustrations with our British friend, Samantha, who felt the same way. Then, ponchos on, we headed into the rain.

If I had to sum up the morning in a word, it would be *mud*. The trail was soggy, but the walk was mostly gentle, with a few uphill stretches. We parted ways with Sam, reconnected at lunch in Salceda, and then said goodbye once more. As we pressed on, we continued to notice just how much the character of the Camino had changed. We were surrounded by large groups of schoolchildren—some loud, many inconsiderate, and most seeming to treat the Camino as more of a group hike than a spiritual journey. The atmosphere was no longer reflective or reverent. It was something else entirely.

Once we passed Arca around midday, the Camino opened up. The crowds thinned. Most pilgrims stop walking by 2:00 p.m., so from that point forward, we had the path almost entirely to ourselves, and we just kept going. Along the way, there was a wire fence where pilgrims had placed crosses made of sticks, almost like a trailside shrine. Pamela asked if we could take a moment and allow her to place a cross on the fence. It was her Cruz de Ferro moment. A little later at Monte do Gozo, five kilometers from Santiago, we stopped at a small chapel to pray. Sitting there, I felt the weight of the journey settle in. The end was near, and the emotion overwhelmed me—I began to weep.

We arrived in Santiago at 7:30 p.m., after walking eleven and a half hours. We walked a marathon: twenty-seven miles. Sure, the New York Marathon probably won't be inviting us anytime soon, but we made it. Along the way, there were stops for coffee, lunch, ice cream, and even bandages. We were exhausted but elated. We had made it.

After taking in the grandeur of the cathedral's exterior, we stepped inside and stayed for the evening Mass. Then we walked to the hotel where Pamela had stayed upon her initial arrival. They didn't have a room, but they did have a small apartment available, which they offered us for the same price. It was a gift. We quickly settled in and slept until ten the next morning. Oh, what a sleep it was!

Her Cross in the Fence

Then Joshua summoned the twelve men whom he had appointed from the Israelites, one from each tribe. Joshua said to them, "Pass on before the ark of the LORD your God into the middle of the Jordan, and each of you take up a stone on his shoulder, according to the number of the tribes of the Israelites, so that this may be a sign among you. When your children ask in time to come, 'What do those stones mean to you?' then you shall tell them that the waters of the Jordan were cut off in front of the ark of the covenant of the LORD. When it crossed over the Jordan, the waters of the Jordan were cut off. So these stones shall be to the Israelites a memorial forever."

—Joshua 4:4–7, NRSVUE

It's fitting that we arrived in Santiago on a day that felt like a day of incredible endurance. It was muddy, rainy, noisy, and long. What we had intended to split into two manageable days became a marathon. Grace doesn't always wait for us to be rested or ready.

Somewhere past Arca, after the crowds had thinned and the Camino had grown quiet, we came across that stretch of wire fence where pilgrims had left crosses. There was no plaque or explanation, just this spontaneous roadside shrine. Pamela stopped. She bent down, gathered two sticks, and wove a cross into the fence. A quiet act of devotion. A small surrender. A sacred moment.

Only later did I realize how much meaning that cross may have carried for her. It wasn't just about the kilometers she had walked. It was about the burdens she had borne beside me for years as the spouse of a clergyperson—the recent season of institutional hurt, the betrayal, the quiet dignity she maintained while watching someone she loved be attacked. It wasn't even just our pain. Our children carried it too, especially our youngest, who witnessed firsthand what spiritual harm can look like. That cross in the fence—it wasn't only hers. In some ways, it was all of ours.

It reminded me of the scene in Joshua, when God instructs the Israelites to gather stones from the Jordan River and set them up as a memorial—so that when future generations ask, "What do these stones mean to you?" there will be a story to tell. The stones themselves weren't holy, but the moment was.

We don't always get to choose where holy things happen. Sometimes they show up in chapels and cathedrals. Sometimes on muddy paths, in waiting rooms, or at bedsides. I was given the gift of being present with both of my parents when they died. Those were places of deep sorrow—but also of startling peace. Of presence. Of holiness. Like the Jordan River. Like a fence on the Camino.

Later that day, at Monte do Gozo, I sat in a small chapel and wept. Not out of pain, but from the sheer weight of the journey, what we had walked, what we had let go, what we had found again. The cross in the fence stayed with me. We made it to the cathedral in Santiago that evening, but that wasn't the first time we stood on holy ground that day.

Reflection Questions:

1. What burdens have your loved ones quietly carried on your behalf? How might you honor their hidden strength?
2. Where have you found holy ground that wasn't a church or sanctuary? How did you recognize God's presence there?

3. What "stones of remembrance" or symbols of grace are you leaving behind for future generations? What story will they tell?

God of memory and meaning,
teach us to mark what matters—
not just with words, but with acts of love, surrender, and hope.
Help us carry one another's burdens with quiet grace,
and to recognize the sacred not only in the destination,
but in the moments we choose to remember.
May the symbols we leave behind tell stories of healing,
and may our lives be signs of your faithfulness
to those who come after us.

Amen.

DAY 38

A Day of Celebration

After easing into the morning, we made our way to the Pilgrim's Office to receive our Certificado. Contrary to how the movie *The Way* portrays it, the process was straightforward. We waited in a long line, filled out a simple form, and were handed our certificates of completion—a quiet but powerful moment marking our arrival in Santiago.

Afterward, we grabbed a light breakfast and headed to the Pilgrim's Mass at noon. The cathedral was packed, not just with pilgrims, but with many tourists as well. Still, the moment was deeply moving. The archbishop was in attendance, and to our great surprise and joy, the *botafumeiro*—the great swinging censer—was used. They typically only swing it on Sundays, so to see it in motion today felt like a special blessing. The oldest document describing the Camino pilgrimage is the twelfth-century *Codex Calixtinus.* The manuscript was stolen in the year 2011, and it was recovered a year later in an electrician's garage. An inside job. So today they were celebrating its return, hence the archbishop's presence.

As the incense from the botafumeiro drifted down over us, I was overwhelmed with a sense of joy and deep gratitude for God's grace, for the strength to complete this journey, and for having Pamela by my side at the end. Pamela was moved to tears as the massive thurible swung above us, a moment we will both remember.

After the Mass, we had lunch and then returned to the cathedral for a guided tour. Later in the afternoon, we wandered out into the plaza to see if we might spot familiar faces—and we did. I introduced Pamela to several of my fellow pilgrims whom I'd met along the way. It brought me great joy to have Pamela meet Camino friends she had only heard about until now.

As I laid down to sleep, I found myself reflecting on the unique nature of this journey. To share something so profound with strangers who quickly become friends—and to know you may never see them again—is both beautiful and bittersweet. There's a quiet sadness that settles in as this chapter comes to a close. I've begun to wonder how I'll transition back into my former role and routines. The Camino changes you—but how exactly, I'll only discover with time.

The Weight of Glory

Now when the priests came out of the holy place (for all the priests who were present had sanctified themselves, without regard to their divisions), all the levitical singers, Asaph, Heman, and Jeduthun, their sons and kindred, arrayed in fine linen, with cymbals, harps, and lyres, stood east of the altar with one hundred twenty priests who were trumpeters, it was the duty of the trumpeters and singers to make themselves heard in unison in praise and thanksgiving to the Lord, *and when the song was raised, with trumpets and cymbals and other musical instruments, in praise to the* Lord, *"For he is good, for his steadfast love endures for ever," the house, the house of the LORD, was filled with a cloud, so that the priests could not stand to minister because of the cloud; for the glory of the LORD filled the house of God.*

—2 Chronicles 5:11–14

I didn't expect to cry during the swinging of the botafumeiro, but as it passed overhead, I looked up through the haze, and something cracked open inside me. I was overwhelmed—not just by the sight but by the weight of what it meant. The smoke rose like the ancient symbol of prayer ascending. As we stood there in the cathedral, it also felt like something was descending: glory, presence, grace. In the Hebrew tradition, the word for glory is *kavod*—the weight of God's nearness. Not a burden, but a blessing so heavy it makes you stop in your tracks.

Pamela wept beside me. I stood silent, stunned by the beauty, by the culmination of so many steps, by the sense that we were no longer remembering something sacred—we were in it. The Camino had been filled with glimpses of the holy, often unexpected. This moment seemed to gather them all. The scent of incense, the soaring music, the echo of prayers in many languages—all of it formed a kind of doxology beyond words.

That night, I lay in bed and thought about how the Camino changes you. You form deep connections with people you may never see again. You weep in churches you've never entered before. You find yourself undone by smoke and song.

Maybe you don't need a swinging censer or a thousand-year-old cathedral to experience kavod. Maybe it comes from watching a couple celebrate fifty years of marriage, or watching a child sleep, or standing under stars you didn't plan to notice. When it arrives, you'll know it. The air thickens. Your breath catches, and for just a moment, everything is still. The memory of that kavod, the glory of God, lasts forever.

Reflection Questions:

1. Can you recall a moment when you felt the weight of God's presence—when the air seemed to thicken with God's glory?
2. How do you respond to mystery in your spiritual life? Do you tend to seek answers, or can you sit with wonder?
3. What symbols, sounds, or rituals have helped you recognize God's nearness in unexpected places?

God of glory and gentle mystery,
thank you for the moments that stop us in our tracks—
when your presence settles like a cloud and we are undone by wonder.
Teach us to welcome mystery without needing to explain it,
to receive grace without needing to deserve it,
and to carry your glory with humility as we return to daily life.
Let the memory of your nearness guide us forward.

Amen.

DAY 39

A Moment of Clarity

Pamela and I attended the Pilgrim's Mass again, partly for the beauty of the ceremony and partly in the hopes of seeing some familiar faces. Once again, to our great surprise and joy, the botafumeiro was used. The president of Spain was in attendance to celebrate the return of the *Codex Calixtinus*. Unfortunately, we didn't spot anyone we knew, so we decided to stroll through the streets of Santiago and enjoy a quiet moment. We stopped for our first cup of coffee of the day, paired with a piece of chocolate cake.

On our way back, I was delighted to spot Hans, a fellow pilgrim, from Ottawa. He's a warm and kind person who has just retired and chose walking the Camino as the way to begin his retirement. His wife, Erica, had joined him on the Camino from Sarria, just as Pamela had joined me. We spent a lovely hour catching up and sharing stories. Hans had also walked to Finisterre and Muxía and highly recommended both places to us. While we were chatting, Andreas and Julia—who had so kindly loaned me her air mattress back in Villamayor—happened to pass by. They stopped to visit with us, which was a pleasant addition to our day.

After wandering some more, Pamela and I had pizza for dinner. During the meal, she noticed a shift in my mood and asked what was bothering me. I shared with her my concerns about my transition back to regular life. This led to a deep conversation about the possibility that our time at our current church might be coming to an end. Though we didn't come to a definitive conclusion, it became clear that there are real questions we need to explore further. Now, we're sitting at a sidewalk café, enjoying a beer and writing in our journals, reflecting on the journey that is behind us, and the journey that still lies ahead.

Grace in the In-Between

By faith Abraham obeyed when he was called to set out for a place that he was to receive as an inheritance; and he set out, not knowing where he was going. By faith he stayed for a time in the land he had been promised, as in a foreign land, living in tents, as did Isaac and Jacob, who were heirs with him of the same promise. For he looked forward to the city that has foundations, whose architect and builder is God. By faith he received power of procreation, even though he was too old—and Sarah herself was barren—because he considered him faithful who had promised.

—Hebrews 11:8–11

Even though we were near the completion of our Camino, on that day in Santiago, we had a feeling of things left unresolved. The journey was over, yet something remained unfinished. It was a day marked by beauty and reunion, yes—but also by a quiet sense of disorientation. The Camino had carried me through valleys of struggle and peaks of joy.

I had experienced grace and forgiveness and offered those things to others in return, yet now standing at the end, I realized I wasn't just walking away from a pilgrimage—I was stepping into another threshold.

We didn't make any decisions that night, but the conversation opened something real. It made space for uncertainty as to the way forward. Though we were unsure what our future held, it was its own kind of sacred space. Not because we had clarity, but because we had honesty. That's often what liminal space requires—not resolution, but reverence. A willingness to linger on the threshold and listen for what's next.

I've come to believe that a life committed to growth will always be a life of transition. It's a rhythm of crossing and recrossing thresholds. The Camino began that way, stepping away from the known, and it ended the same way, with new questions emerging from what I thought would be closure. The gift is that there's grace in the in-between. Theologians have long described the Kingdom of God as already and not yet. In Christ—and through the Spirit given to the Church—the Kingdom has come. It is here, present, and at work. Yet God's Kingdom is not here in its fullness. We live in the tension between what has been revealed and what is still unfolding.

Our lives reflect that same rhythm. We are already walking in grace but not yet in completion. We live by faith in what is becoming, even as we give thanks for what already is. Martin Luther once likened our lives to a printing press. The type is set, letter by letter, line by line, but we cannot always read it while it's still on the tray. Only when the page is printed do we see what has truly been written. In the same way, the fullness of what God is doing in and through our lives often remains hidden until it's revealed in time. We walk forward, not always knowing how the story will read, but trusting the Author.

That day reminded me that the journey isn't something we finish. It's something we carry forward. Liminal space doesn't mean God is absent—it means God is inviting us to walk by trust, not sight. Sometimes, the greatest act of faith is to admit, "I don't know what's next, but I trust that grace will meet me there."

Reflection Questions:

1. What "commas" have you mistaken for periods—times when you thought a journey had ended but something deeper was just beginning?
2. Who in your life has helped you notice what's stirring beneath the surface when you couldn't name it yourself?
3. What threshold might you be standing on right now? How is God inviting you to listen, linger, or lean in?

God of the threshold,
you meet us in the spaces where clarity is absent
but grace is near.
When the road ends and a new path begins,
give us courage to pause, to listen, to trust.
Help us welcome the questions that linger,
and walk forward not by sight, but by faith—
believing that you are already where we're going.

Amen.

DAY 40

Camino Connections at the End of the World

Pamela and I took a bus to Finisterre, which means "the end of the world." Finisterre is situated at the westernmost point of continental Europe. Finisterre has long held symbolic meaning for pilgrims on the Camino. The drive itself was stunning, winding through the lush hills and coastal views of Galicia. Along the way, we found ourselves dreaming aloud about returning someday to walk from Santiago to both Finisterre and Muxía.

A long tradition of the Camino is for pilgrims to burn the clothing they walked in when they arrive in Finisterre. When we stood on the cliff overlooking the Atlantic Ocean, we realized that as non-smokers, we didn't have any matches or a lighter. Once again, fellow pilgrims to the rescue. I didn't burn all my clothes, but I never wanted to wear the T-shirt I wore on the Camino again. So, with the assistance of my fellow pilgrim, I watched it go up in flames. Pamela joined the celebration, throwing in her socks as well. Our Camino was now complete.

But what made the day truly unforgettable was the unexpected reunion with so many Camino friends. As soon as we stepped off the bus, we ran into Elizabeth from California and Gary from Australia, just as they were heading back to Santiago. Not long after, I recognized two young South Korean women I'd met earlier on the trail. Later that afternoon, we found Mona from the Netherlands and reminisced and reflected on our journeys.

After checking into our room, we stepped outside, and there, as if by something stronger than fate, were Barbara and Jordan from Austin. It was almost surreal. Barbara thanked Pamela for "sharing me" with the Camino community for a month. She shared that Jordan's time with Father Tony, Mary, and me had been some of the most meaningful of his Camino. It felt good—deeply good—to know that I had made a lasting impact, even while traveling in an "undercover" role.

Then, just down the street, we bumped into Kim and Scott from California. The Camino keeps weaving these beautiful threads of connection. Pamela was finally able to meet nearly all of the fellow pilgrims I had journeyed with over the past month, each of whom had left an imprint on my experience. Only a few key friends were missing, but the sense of closure was real and deeply satisfying.

As our time in Finisterre drew to a close, it truly felt like the closing chapter of a sacred and transformative story. The Camino has given more than I could have imagined—and definitely more than I deserved, the very definition of grace.

At the End of the World

On this mountain the LORD of hosts will make for all peoples a feast of rich food, a feast of well-aged wines, of rich food filled with marrow, of well-aged wines strained clear. And he will destroy on this mountain the shroud that is cast over all peoples, the covering that is spread over all nations; he will swallow up death forever. Then the Lord GOD *will wipe away the tears from all faces, and the disgrace of his people he will take away from all the earth, for the* LORD *has spoken. It will be said on that day, "See, this is our God; we have waited for him, so that he might save us. This is the* LORD *for whom we have waited; let us be glad and rejoice in his salvation."*

—Isaiah 25:6–9, NRSVUE

The journey to Finisterre echoed the paradox of the Christian story: endings that are also beginnings. Crosses that lead to life. Goodbyes that hint at reunion. A destination that becomes a doorway.

What struck me most about that day wasn't just the breathtaking landscape or the symbolism of arriving at land's end—it was the unexpected joy of reunion. One by one, fellow pilgrims appeared like characters returning for the final act of a play.

Each encounter carried a weight of significance. It wasn't just nostalgia. It was fulfillment. A glimpse of what Scripture calls the communion of saints—a foretaste of that promised day when we will know fully, even as we are fully known. These weren't just companions from the trail. They were witnesses to a shared transformation. There's something profoundly holy about being known—not for your title or credentials, but simply for who you are. That, too, felt eschatological—a glimpse of the day when we will stand before God and one another with nothing left to hide, and nothing left to prove.

The word *apocalypse* in its Ancient Greek usage means revelation or unveiling. That is what this final day felt like. In small ways and sacred conversations, what had been hidden was gently revealed. Not just my vocation, but my impact. Not just my identity, but my belonging. That day, in conversations and laughter, I found myself more revealed than I had been throughout the Camino. I had walked for weeks in relative anonymity, and it had been freeing. As the journey ended, however, there was also a quiet grace in no longer needing to remain hidden. In being seen, known, and still welcomed.

There was also feasting—not grand or formal, but rich in fellowship. The end of the Camino didn't bring answers so much as clarity. The road didn't conclude in solitude—it concluded in communion. The feast, the friends, the conversations, they all pointed toward something deeper. A sacred pattern. That's the shape of the Kingdom: reunion, revelation, joy. Though I stood at the edge of the continent, I sensed I was not at the end of anything but on the threshold of something eternal.

Reflection Questions:

1. Where in your own life have you experienced an "ending" that also felt like a beginning?

2. When have you felt most deeply seen and known, not for what you do, but for who you are?

3. The word *apocalypse* means unveiling. What has recently been unveiled in your life—about your purpose, your relationships, or your faith?

Lord of all our journeys,
You meet us at the thresholds of life—
not with an ending, but with a new beginning.
You gather us with companions old and new,
weaving our stories into a tapestry of grace.
Thank you for the gift of being seen and known,
for the table of friendship and the promise of reunion.
As we step from what has been into what will be,
keep our hearts open to your Kingdom's shape—
reunion, revelation, joy—
until we stand together at your eternal feast.

Amen.

EPILOGUE

To Walk It Back

The Camino Ends. Life Continues.

What I didn't fully realize at the time was that the Camino's greatest challenge wasn't the mountains or the Meseta—it was the return. The slow reentry into ordinary life with an extraordinary heart. That's where the real pilgrimage begins. There's a sacred impermanence to the Camino. Each day brought new faces, new paths, new aches, and unexpected gifts. That rhythm, beautiful as it was, could never be sustained forever. You're not meant to live on the trail. The Camino is temporary. Life at home—marriage, family, parish, vocation—that's where transformation is tested and lived.

Over time, I've come to see that permanence is the place where lasting transformation takes root. The Benedictines speak of three vows: conversion, stability, and obedience. These vows are deeply countercultural—and deeply needed. The Camino gave me conversion: a healing of old wounds, a re-centering of purpose, a rediscovery of joy. What the Camino initiated, stability and obedience must now sustain. Stability means choosing a place, a community. It's the holy refusal to keep chasing novelty. Obedience, from the Latin *ob-audire*, means to listen, not to control or conform, but to attend with love. To listen for God in Scripture, in the Church, in one another.

Real growth—soul-deep, enduring growth—rarely comes from the next adventure. It comes from the long listening: to your spouse across the table, to your parish in its complexity, to the Spirit whispering through pain or joy. It comes from telling the truth. From staying when staying is hard. Stability in relationships is the thing that allows us to be vulnerable, knowing that when we reveal the deep things of our heart, we won't be rejected.

I still carry the Camino with me. I still carry the people who shaped it. Some friendships faded like campfires—beautiful, warm, and brief. Others surprised me by continuing: messages across time zones, a care package from Kim and Scott with bottles of Simi wine, reunions that reminded me the Camino was never just mine. Pamela and I were blessed to visit Father Tony in Dallas during one of his furloughs from Moscow. We toured Sonoma Valley with Kim and Scott after a wedding in California. We've been blessed to share time with Barbara and her husband, Russ, more than once back home in Texas.

But the story that perhaps best reflects the Camino's lasting reach happened in Virginia: Barbara's son, Jordan, and Maura's daughter, Mary, who met on the trail, fell in love and were married four years later. Pamela and I were honored to attend their wedding, and I was even asked to read Scripture during the service. It was a mini-Camino reunion. Grace does that: It continues, multiplies, and surprises.

For those who might be wondering—yes, I did return to my parish after the Camino and continued to serve there for another five years. After fourteen years in that congregation, I sensed it was time for a new challenge. One of the great joys I carried from the Camino was a renewed love for working with young people. So, after twenty-six years in parish ministry, I stepped away and accepted a position as Chaplain at an Episcopal school, where I ministered to students ranging from three-year-olds to high school seniors.

After many rich and fulfilling years at the school, I retired, at least for a while. Nine months into retirement, my bishop called to ask if I'd consider serving part-time as an interim rector for a nearby parish. I said yes. At the time, I thought I was simply stepping in to help a congregation in transition. What I didn't fully realize was that his invitation was also a gift—a quiet act of trust that reached deeper than I expected.

Being asked by my bishop to serve this community—one that had weathered its own heartache—became not only a ministry of healing for them, but also a powerful sacrament of redemption for me. It was during my time there, while preparing a presentation on the Camino for a local civic group, that the idea for this book was born. The blessing of sharing my Camino story with others is that in my mind's eye, I get to walk the Camino once more, with all my Camino buddies beside me. These connections, whether enduring or fleeting, are now woven into the story I live each day.

Buen Camino!